JavaScript Unleashed: Harnessing the Power of Web Scripting

Kameron Hussain and Frahaan Hussain

Published by Sonar Publishing, 2023.

While every precaution has been taken in the preparation of this book, the publisher assumes no responsibility for errors or omissions, or for damages resulting from the use of the information contained herein.

JAVASCRIPT UNLEASHED: HARNESSING THE POWER OF WEB SCRIPTING

First edition. November 12, 2023.

Copyright © 2023 Kameron Hussain and Frahaan Hussain.

ISBN: 979-8223134053

Written by Kameron Hussain and Frahaan Hussain.

Table of Contents

ASSISTANT

User Interface (UI) Design

Responsive Design

Component-Based Development

State Management

Performance Optimization

Frontend Testing

Accessibility

Cross-Browser Compatibility

Internationalization (i18n) and Localization (l10n)

Progressive Web App (PWA)

Section 17.3: Backend Development

Technology Stack

Server Setup

API Design

Data Management

Authentication and Authorization

Middleware

Testing and Debugging

Scalability and Performance

API Security

3. Advanced JavaScript

4. Front-End Libraries and Frameworks

5. Server-Side JavaScript

6. Data Handling and Visualization

7. Security and Best Practices

8. Testing and Debugging

9. Single-Page Applications (SPAs)

10. Mobile App Development

11. Web Performance Optimization

12. Accessibility

13. Internationalization and Localization

14. Advanced JavaScript Topics

15. Real-World Project

16. JavaScript Trends and Future

17. Tips for JavaScript Developers

18. Conclusion and Beyond

Section 20.2: The Journey of Becoming a JavaScript Expert

1. Master the Fundamentals

2. Explore Advanced Topics

3. Build Real-World Projects

4. Deepen Your Web Development Skills

5. Explore Frameworks and Libraries

6. Practice Problem Solving

7. Contribute to Open Source

8. Stay Updated

9. Peer Collaboration and Code Reviews

10. Teach and Share Knowledge

11. Networking and Community Involvement

12. Adapt to Industry Trends

13. Certifications and Formal Education

14. Continuous Learning

Section 20.3: Embracing Change in Web Development

1. Keep Learning New Technologies

2. Follow Industry Trends

3. Attend Conferences and Meetups

4. Engage with Online Communities

5. Regularly Update Your Skills

6. Experiment with New Features

7. Stay Security Conscious

8. Adopt Agile and DevOps Practices

9. Learn from Mistakes

10. Collaborate and Seek Feedback

11. Build a Personal Brand

12. Explore Cross-Platform Development

13. Adapt to Browser Updates

14. Migrate Legacy Code

15. Embrace the JavaScript Ecosystem

16. Enjoy the Journey

Section 20.4: Your Next Steps as a JavaScript Developer

1. Specialize or Diversify

2. Build a Portfolio

3. Open Source Contributions

4. Continued Learning

5. Networking

6. Job Search and Freelancing

7. Certifications

8. Stay Updated

9. Soft Skills

10. Mentorship

11. Side Projects

12. Consider Advanced Topics

13. Contribute to the Community

14. Evaluate Job Offers

15. Set Goals

Section 20.5: Thank You and Acknowledgments

Chapter 1: Introduction to JavaScript

1.1 What Is JavaScript?

JavaScript is a versatile and widely used programming language in web development. It is primarily known for adding interactivity and dynamic behavior to web pages. In this section, we'll delve into the fundamentals of JavaScript and understand its role in modern web development.

JavaScript is a high-level, interpreted scripting language. This means that you can write code in JavaScript and execute it directly in web browsers without the need for compilation. It's commonly embedded within HTML documents and runs on the client side, allowing you to create interactive web applications.

JavaScript's Core Features

JavaScript provides a rich set of features that make it a powerful language for web development:

1. **Variables and Data Types:** JavaScript supports various data types, including numbers, strings, booleans, and objects. You can declare variables to store and manipulate data.
2. **Functions:** Functions are reusable blocks of code that can be defined and called throughout your program. They are crucial for organizing and modularizing your code.
3. **Control Structures:** JavaScript supports conditional statements like if, else, and switch, as well as looping structures like for, while, and do-while.
4. **Objects and Prototypes:** JavaScript is an object-oriented language, and objects are central to its design. Objects can

have properties and methods, and you can create custom objects and prototypes.

5. **Event Handling:** JavaScript enables you to respond to user interactions and events on web pages, such as mouse clicks and keyboard input.

6. **DOM Manipulation:** The Document Object Model (DOM) represents the structure of HTML documents in a tree-like fashion. JavaScript can interact with and manipulate the DOM to change the content and appearance of web pages dynamically.

7. **Asynchronous Programming:** JavaScript supports asynchronous operations using callbacks, promises, and async/await, allowing you to perform tasks like fetching data from servers without blocking the user interface.

The Role of JavaScript in Web Development

JavaScript plays a pivotal role in modern web development:

- **Enhanced User Experience:** It enables developers to create dynamic and responsive user interfaces, improving the overall user experience.

- **Client-Side Interactivity:** JavaScript executes in the user's browser, reducing the need for server round-trips, which makes web applications feel more responsive.

- **Web Applications:** JavaScript powers many web applications, from social media platforms to online editors, by handling complex functionality.

- **Frameworks and Libraries:** A wide range of JavaScript frameworks and libraries, such as React, Angular, and

Vue.js, have emerged to simplify and streamline web development.

In the next sections of this chapter, we'll explore the history of JavaScript, why it matters, and how to set up your development environment to start writing JavaScript code. Get ready to embark on a journey into the world of JavaScript!

1.2 A Brief History of JavaScript

JavaScript has a fascinating history that has shaped it into the versatile language it is today. In this section, we'll take a journey through the key milestones and events that have contributed to the development of JavaScript.

Origins in Netscape

JavaScript was originally developed by Brendan Eich while he was working at Netscape Communications Corporation in the early 1990s. The initial goal was to create a scripting language for web browsers to make web pages more interactive. In September 1995, Netscape released JavaScript as part of Netscape Navigator 2.0, marking the birth of JavaScript.

The Birth of ECMAScript

To standardize JavaScript, Netscape submitted it to the European Computer Manufacturers Association (ECMA) in 1996. This standardization effort led to the creation of ECMAScript, a specification that defines the core features of JavaScript. ECMAScript 1, the first official version of the specification, was released in June 1997. Subsequent versions, such as ECMAScript 3 (1999) and ECMAScript 5 (2009), introduced important features and improvements.

The Browser Wars and DOM

During the late 1990s and early 2000s, the web experienced the "Browser Wars" between Netscape Navigator and Microsoft Internet Explorer. This competition led to rapid advancements in web technologies, including JavaScript. Both browsers introduced their own enhancements and proprietary features.

In parallel, the Document Object Model (DOM) emerged as a crucial component of web development. The DOM provided a standardized way to interact with the structure and content of web documents, enabling dynamic changes to web pages. JavaScript played a central role in manipulating the DOM to create dynamic user interfaces.

AJAX and Web 2.0

In the mid-2000s, a technique known as Asynchronous JavaScript and XML (AJAX) gained prominence. AJAX allowed web applications to exchange data with servers in the background without requiring a full page refresh. This marked a significant shift in web development, enabling the creation of more responsive and interactive web applications. AJAX was instrumental in the development of Web 2.0 applications.

The Rise of JavaScript Libraries and Frameworks

As web applications became more complex, developers sought ways to streamline development. This led to the emergence of JavaScript libraries and frameworks. jQuery, released in 2006, became immensely popular for simplifying DOM manipulation and cross-browser compatibility.

In subsequent years, frameworks like AngularJS (later Angular), React, and Vue.js revolutionized front-end development, offering structured approaches to building web applications.

The Current Landscape

Today, JavaScript is one of the most widely used programming languages in the world. It powers not only web applications but also server-side development through platforms like Node.js. The language continues to evolve with regular updates to the ECMAScript specification, introducing features that enhance developer productivity and application performance.

In the next section, we'll explore why JavaScript matters and its relevance in the modern web development landscape. Understanding its history provides valuable context for appreciating the language's growth and capabilities.

1.3 Why JavaScript Matters

JavaScript's significance in the world of web development cannot be overstated. In this section, we'll explore the reasons why JavaScript matters and why it continues to be a vital technology in the modern web landscape.

1. Versatility and Ubiquity

JavaScript is a versatile language that runs in web browsers, making it ubiquitous. Every major web browser, including Google Chrome, Mozilla Firefox, Microsoft Edge, and Apple Safari, supports JavaScript. This ubiquity ensures that JavaScript-powered web applications can reach a vast audience without requiring users to install additional software.

2. Enhancing User Experience

JavaScript enables developers to create rich, interactive, and dynamic user interfaces. Features like smooth animations, real-time updates, and interactive forms enhance the user experience. With JavaScript, web applications can mimic the responsiveness and interactivity of traditional desktop applications.

```javascript
// Example of simple animation using JavaScript

const element = document.getElementById("animated-element");

element.style.transition = "transform 1s";

element.addEventListener("click", () => {

element.style.transform = "translateX(100px)";

});
```

3. Asynchronous Communication

JavaScript's asynchronous capabilities are crucial for building modern web applications. With techniques like AJAX (Asynchronous JavaScript and XML) and the Fetch API, web applications can send and receive data from servers without blocking the user interface. This asynchronous behavior allows for real-time updates and a smoother user experience.

```javascript
// Example of making an asynchronous HTTP request with Fetch API

fetch("https://api.example.com/data")

.then((response) => response.json())

.then((data) => {
```

```
console.log(data);

})

.catch((error) => {

console.error("Error:", error);

});
```

4. Cross-Platform Compatibility

JavaScript's ability to run in web browsers across different platforms and devices makes it a valuable tool for cross-platform development. Whether users access a web application from a desktop computer, tablet, or smartphone, JavaScript ensures a consistent experience.

5. Ecosystem and Community

JavaScript has a vast and active developer community. This community has created a rich ecosystem of libraries, frameworks, and tools that simplify and accelerate web development. Popular libraries like jQuery, and powerful frameworks like React and Angular, have significantly contributed to the ecosystem's growth.

6. Server-Side Development

In addition to client-side web development, JavaScript has expanded its reach to server-side development through technologies like Node.js. This allows developers to use JavaScript for both the front-end and back-end, enabling full-stack development with a single language.

7. Continuous Evolution

JavaScript is not a stagnant language. It continues to evolve with regular updates to the ECMAScript specification. These updates introduce new features and improvements, helping developers write cleaner and more efficient code. Features like arrow functions, async/await, and module imports have enhanced developer productivity.

8. Career Opportunities

Proficiency in JavaScript opens doors to a wide range of career opportunities. Web development remains a high-demand field, and JavaScript developers are sought after by companies of all sizes. Whether you aspire to work as a front-end developer, full-stack developer, or specialize in a particular JavaScript framework, the skills you gain in JavaScript are valuable in the job market.

In summary, JavaScript matters because it empowers developers to create interactive and engaging web applications, offers cross-platform compatibility, enjoys a robust ecosystem, and continues to evolve to meet the demands of modern web development. Its importance in the tech industry is undeniable, and learning JavaScript is a valuable step for anyone interested in web development.

1.4 Setting Up Your Development Environment

Before you start writing JavaScript code, it's essential to set up your development environment. In this section, we'll walk through the steps to prepare your development environment to work with JavaScript effectively.

1. Text Editor or Integrated Development

Environment (IDE)

The first decision you'll need to make is choosing a text editor or integrated development environment (IDE) for writing JavaScript code. Some popular options include:

- **Visual Studio Code (VS Code):** A free, open-source code editor with excellent JavaScript support, including extensions for debugging and linting.

- **Sublime Text:** A lightweight and highly customizable text editor with a strong developer community and many JavaScript-related packages.

- **Atom:** Another free, open-source text editor with extensive customization options and JavaScript support through packages.

- **WebStorm:** A commercial IDE designed specifically for web development, including robust JavaScript tools and features.

Choose the one that suits your preferences and workflow best. Many developers prefer VS Code for its versatility, but the choice ultimately depends on your needs.

2. Web Browser

Since JavaScript primarily runs in web browsers, having a modern web browser installed is essential for testing and debugging your code. Popular web browsers like Google Chrome, Mozilla Firefox, Microsoft Edge, and Apple Safari all have built-in developer tools for inspecting and debugging JavaScript.

3. Node.js (Optional)

While JavaScript is commonly associated with web browsers, Node.js allows you to run JavaScript on the server-side. Depending on your project requirements, you might want to install Node.js and npm (Node Package Manager). Node.js is particularly useful for building server-side applications and automating tasks with JavaScript.

4. Version Control System (Optional)

Using a version control system like Git is highly recommended, especially if you're working on collaborative projects or want to keep track of changes in your code. You can install Git and use it alongside your text editor or IDE to manage your codebase efficiently.

5. Browser Extensions

Consider installing browser extensions that can assist you in web development. For example, browser extensions like "React Developer Tools" or "Redux DevTools" are helpful when working with specific JavaScript libraries or frameworks. These tools provide insights into the component hierarchy and state management, making debugging easier.

6. Code Linters and Formatters

To maintain clean and consistent code, consider using code linters and formatters. Popular JavaScript linters like ESLint and JSHint help you identify and fix code style issues and potential errors. Additionally, code formatters like Prettier can automatically format your code according to predefined rules.

7. JavaScript Frameworks and Libraries

Depending on your project, you might need to install specific JavaScript frameworks or libraries. Many of them can be added to your project using npm or included directly from content delivery networks (CDNs).

For example, to use React for building user interfaces, you can install it with npm:

npm install react react-dom

Alternatively, you can include React via CDN links in your HTML file.

8. Setting Up a Local Development Server

When working on web applications, it's often beneficial to run a local development server. This ensures that your JavaScript code behaves as expected in a web environment. Tools like http-server or live-server can serve your web files locally and provide features like auto-reloading when changes are detected.

npm install -g http-server

9. Learning Resources

Finally, gather learning resources such as books, tutorials, online courses, and documentation. JavaScript has a vast and supportive community, and there are numerous resources available for beginners and experienced developers alike.

With your development environment set up, you're ready to begin your journey into JavaScript. In the next section, we'll guide you through writing your first JavaScript program, so you can start experimenting with the language and its capabilities.

1.5 Your First JavaScript Program

Now that you have your development environment set up, it's time to write your first JavaScript program. In this section, we'll guide you through the process step by step.

1. Create an HTML File

To begin, create an HTML file where you can include your JavaScript code. You can use a text editor like Visual Studio Code to create a new file and save it with an ".html" extension. For example, you can name it "index.html."

```
<!DOCTYPE html>

<html lang="en">

<head>

<meta charset="UTF-8">

<meta name="viewport" content="width=device-width, initial-scale=1.0">

<title>My First JavaScript Program</title>

</head>

<body>

<h1>Hello, JavaScript!</h1>

<p>This is my first JavaScript program.</p>

<script src="script.js"></script>

</body>
```

```
</html>
```

In this HTML file, we have a simple structure with a title, a heading, and a paragraph. We also include a <script> tag to reference an external JavaScript file called "script.js," which we will create in the next step.

2. Create a JavaScript File

Next, create a JavaScript file named "script.js" in the same directory as your HTML file. This is where you will write your JavaScript code.

```
// script.js

// This is a single-line comment

/*

This is a multi-line comment.

You can add comments to explain your code.

*/

// Display a message in the browser's console

console.log("Hello, JavaScript!");

// Alert a message in a pop-up dialog

alert("Welcome to JavaScript!");
```

In this JavaScript file, we start by adding comments. Comments are essential for explaining your code and providing context to yourself and other developers.

We use console.log() to print a message to the browser's console, which is a useful tool for debugging and inspecting JavaScript code. The alert() function displays a pop-up dialog with a message.

3. Link JavaScript to HTML

To connect your JavaScript file to your HTML document, make sure you include the <script> tag with the src attribute pointing to your "script.js" file, as shown in the HTML code above. This tells the browser to load and execute your JavaScript code.

4. Open in a Web Browser

Now, open your "index.html" file in a web browser. You can do this by right-clicking the file and selecting "Open with" or simply dragging the file into your browser window.

You should see your HTML content displayed with the heading "Hello, JavaScript!" and the paragraph below it. Additionally, you'll notice that the JavaScript code you wrote in "script.js" has executed. You may see the message "Hello, JavaScript!" printed in the browser's console, and an alert dialog with the message "Welcome to JavaScript!" will appear.

Congratulations! You've successfully written and executed your first JavaScript program. This simple example demonstrates how JavaScript can interact with web pages and enhance their functionality. You're now ready to explore JavaScript further and begin building more complex web applications.

Chapter 2: JavaScript Basics

2.1 Variables and Data Types

In JavaScript, variables are fundamental for storing and managing data. Understanding variables and data types is a crucial first step in your journey to mastering JavaScript.

1. Variable Declaration

In JavaScript, you declare variables using the var, let, or const keywords. Here's how you can declare variables:

// Using 'var' (historical, not recommended)

var age = 30;

// Using 'let' (preferred for mutable variables)

let name = "John";

// Using 'const' (preferred for constants)

const pi = 3.1415;

- var has historically been used to declare variables, but it has some quirks and is generally avoided in modern JavaScript.

- let is the preferred choice for declaring mutable variables. You can change the value assigned to a let variable.

- const is used for declaring constants, and its value cannot be changed once assigned.

2. Data Types

JavaScript has several built-in data types, including:

- **Number:** Represents numeric values, both integers and floating-point numbers. For example:

let age = 30;

let price = 19.99;

- **String:** Represents text and is enclosed in single (") or double ("") quotes. For example:

let name = "John";

let message = 'Hello, World!';

- **Boolean:** Represents true or false values. For example:

let isStudent = **true**;

let hasAccount = **false**;

- **Undefined:** Represents a variable that has been declared but hasn't been assigned a value. For example:

let firstName;

console.log(firstName); // *Outputs: undefined*

- **Null:** Represents the intentional absence of any object value. For example:

let emptyValue = **null**;

- **Object:** Represents a collection of key-value pairs, where keys are strings (or symbols) and values can be of any data type. For example:

```
let person = {

name: "Alice",

age: 25,

isStudent: true,

};
```

- **Array:** Represents an ordered list of values, typically of the same data type. For example:

```
let colors = ["red", "green", "blue"];

let scores = [98, 85, 72, 91];
```

- **Function:** Represents a reusable block of code. Functions can take parameters and return values. For example:

```
function add(a, b) {

return a + b;

}
```

3. Variable Assignment and Reassignment

You can assign values to variables using the assignment operator =:

```
let age = 30;
```

```
let name = "John";
```

Variables can also be reassigned with new values:

```
let score = 85; // Initial assignment
```

```
score = 92; // Reassignment
```

4. Variable Naming Rules

When naming variables in JavaScript:

- Variable names are case-sensitive (myVariable is not the same as myvariable).

- Variable names can only contain letters, digits, underscores, or dollar signs.

- Variable names must start with a letter, underscore, or dollar sign (not a digit).

- Reserved words like if, for, and function cannot be used as variable names.

5. Dynamic Typing

JavaScript is a dynamically typed language, which means that variables can change their data type during runtime. For example:

```
let value = 42; // 'value' is a number
```

```
value = "Hello"; // Now 'value' is a string
```

```
value = true; // And now 'value' is a boolean
```

Understanding variables and data types is the foundation for working with JavaScript. In the next sections of this chapter, we'll explore how to perform operations on variables, work with operators and expressions, and control the flow of your code with conditional statements.

2.2 Operators and Expressions

Operators in JavaScript are symbols or keywords used to perform operations on operands. Operands can be variables, values, or expressions. Understanding operators is essential for performing various calculations and operations in your JavaScript code.

1. Arithmetic Operators

Arithmetic operators are used for basic mathematical operations:

- **Addition (+):** Adds two values together.

let sum = 5 + 3; // *sum is 8*

- **Subtraction (-):** Subtracts the right operand from the left operand.

let difference = 10 - 4; // *difference is 6*

- **Multiplication (*):** Multiplies two values.

let product = 6 * 7; // *product is 42*

- **Division (/):** Divides the left operand by the right operand.

let quotient = 20 / 4; // *quotient is 5*

- **Modulus (%):** Returns the remainder of the division of the left operand by the right operand.

let remainder = 17 % 5; // *remainder is 2*

2. Assignment Operators

Assignment operators are used to assign values to variables:

- **Assignment (=):** Assigns the value on the right to the variable on the left.

let x = 10;

- **Addition Assignment (+=):** Adds the right operand to the variable on the left and assigns the result to the left operand.

let y = 5;

y += 3; // *y is now 8*

- **Subtraction Assignment (-=):** Subtracts the right operand from the variable on the left and assigns the result to the left operand.

let z = 15;

z -= 4; // *z is now 11*

- **Multiplication Assignment (*=):** Multiplies the variable on the left by the right operand and assigns the result to the left operand.

let w = 7;

w *= 2; // *w is now 14*

• **Division Assignment** (/=): Divides the variable on the left by the right operand and assigns the result to the left operand.

let a = 20;

a /= 5; // *a is now 4*

3. Comparison Operators

Comparison operators are used to compare values and return a Boolean (true or false) result:

• **Equal** (==): Checks if two values are equal, but it performs type coercion (converts values to the same type).

let isEqual = 5 == "5"; // *isEqual is true*

• **Not Equal** (!=): Checks if two values are not equal (with type coercion).

let isNotEqual = 10 != "5"; // *isNotEqual is false*

• **Strict Equal** (===): Checks if two values are equal without type coercion (must be the same type and have the same value).

let isStrictEqual = 5 === 5; // *isStrictEqual is true*

• **Strict Not Equal** (!==): Checks if two values are not equal without type coercion.

let isStrictNotEqual = 10 !== "5"; // *isStrictNotEqual is true*

- **Greater Than (>):** Checks if the left operand is greater than the right operand.

let isGreaterThan = 8 > 3; *// isGreaterThan is true*

- **Less Than (<):** Checks if the left operand is less than the right operand.

let isLessThan = 4 < 7; *// isLessThan is true*

- **Greater Than or Equal (>=):** Checks if the left operand is greater than or equal to the right operand.

let isGreaterOrEqual = 5 >= 5; *// isGreaterOrEqual is true*

- **Less Than or Equal (<=):** Checks if the left operand is less than or equal to the right operand.

let isLessOrEqual = 3 <= 3; *// isLessOrEqual is true*

4. Logical Operators

Logical operators are used to perform logical operations and return a Boolean result:

- **Logical AND (&&):** Returns true if both operands are true.

let isBothTrue = **true** && **true**; *// isBothTrue is true*

- **Logical OR (||):** Returns true if at least one operand is true.

let isEitherTrue = **true** || **false**; *// isEitherTrue is true*

- **Logical NOT (!):** Returns the opposite Boolean value of the operand.

let isNotTrue = **!true**; *// isNotTrue is false*

These are some of the most commonly used operators in JavaScript. They allow you to perform a wide range of operations, from basic arithmetic calculations to complex logical evaluations. Understanding how to use operators is fundamental for writing JavaScript code that can manipulate and process data effectively. In the following sections, we'll explore control structures, such as conditional statements and loops, which allow you to make decisions and repeat actions in your code.

2.3 Control Structures: if, else, and switch

Control structures in JavaScript are essential for determining the flow of your code. They allow you to make decisions and execute different blocks of code based on conditions. In this section, we'll explore the if, else, and switch statements, which are fundamental for controlling the behavior of your JavaScript programs.

1. The if Statement

The if statement is used to execute a block of code if a specified condition is true. Here's the basic syntax:

if (condition) {

// Code to execute if the condition is true

}

For example, you can use an if statement to check if a user is old enough to access a certain website:

```
const age = 18;

if (age >= 18) {

console.log("You are old enough to access this website.");

}
```

In this example, the code inside the if block is executed because the condition age >= 18 is true.

2. The else Statement

The else statement is used in conjunction with if to execute a different block of code if the if condition is false. Here's how it works:

```
if (condition) {

// Code to execute if the condition is true

} else {

// Code to execute if the condition is false

}
```

For example, you can modify the previous example to display a message for users who are not old enough:

```
const age = 16;

if (age >= 18) {

console.log("You are old enough to access this website.");

} else {

console.log("You are not old enough to access this website.");
```

```
}
```

In this case, since age is 16, the code inside the else block is executed.

3. The else if Statement

You can use the else if statement to check multiple conditions sequentially after an initial if statement. Here's the syntax:

```
if (condition1) {

// Code to execute if condition1 is true

} else if (condition2) {

// Code to execute if condition2 is true

} else {

// Code to execute if none of the conditions are true

}
```

For example, you can use else if to categorize users based on their age:

```
const age = 25;

if (age < 18) {

console.log("You are a minor.");

} else if (age >= 18 && age < 65) {

console.log("You are an adult.");

} else {

console.log("You are a senior citizen.");
```

```
}
```

In this example, the code inside the second if block is executed because the condition age >= 18 && age < 65 is true.

4. The switch Statement

The switch statement is used when you want to select one of many code blocks to be executed. It's often used when you have a single value that can have multiple cases. Here's the basic syntax:

```
switch (expression) {

case value1:

// Code to execute if expression equals value1

break;

case value2:

// Code to execute if expression equals value2

break;

// Add more cases as needed

default:

// Code to execute if none of the cases match expression

}
```

Here's an example of using a switch statement to determine the day of the week based on a number:

```
const dayNumber = 3;

let dayName;
```

```
switch (dayNumber) {

case 1:

dayName = "Monday";

break;

case 2:

dayName = "Tuesday";

break;

case 3:

dayName = "Wednesday";

break;

case 4:

dayName = "Thursday";

break;

case 5:

dayName = "Friday";

break;

case 6:

dayName = "Saturday";

break;

case 7:
```

dayName = "Sunday";

break;

default:

dayName = "Invalid day number";

}

console.log(`Today is ${dayName}.`);

In this example, the switch statement evaluates dayNumber, and the corresponding case is executed based on its value. If none of the cases match, the default block is executed.

Control structures like if, else, and switch are crucial for adding logic and decision-making capabilities to your JavaScript programs. They allow your code to adapt and respond to different situations, making your applications more powerful and dynamic.

2.4 Loops: for, while, and do-while

Loops are essential in programming for executing a block of code repeatedly. JavaScript provides three main types of loops: for, while, and do-while. In this section, we'll explore how to use these loops to efficiently repeat tasks.

1. The for Loop

The for loop is commonly used when you know how many times you want to execute a block of code. It has three parts: initialization, condition, and iteration.

Here's the basic syntax of a for loop:

```
for (initialization; condition; iteration) {

// Code to be executed repeatedly

}
```

For example, you can use a for loop to print numbers from 1 to 5:

```
for (let i = 1; i <= 5; i++) {

console.log(i);

}
```

In this example: - let i = 1 initializes a variable i to 1. - i <= 5 is the condition that checks whether i is less than or equal to 5. - i++ is the iteration step, which increments i by 1 in each iteration.

The loop will run as long as the condition i <= 5 is true, and it prints the values of i from 1 to 5.

2. The while Loop

The while loop is used when you don't know in advance how many times you need to execute a block of code. It relies on a condition to control the loop's execution.

Here's the basic syntax of a while loop:

```
while (condition) {

// Code to be executed repeatedly

}
```

For example, you can use a while loop to print numbers from 1 to 5:

```
let i = 1;
```

```javascript
while (i <= 5) {

console.log(i);

i++;

}
```

In this example: - let i = 1 initializes a variable i to 1 before the loop. - i <= 5 is the condition that checks whether i is less than or equal to 5. - i++ is used to increment i within the loop.

The loop continues to run as long as the condition i <= 5 is true.

3. The do-while Loop

The do-while loop is similar to the while loop, but it ensures that the block of code is executed at least once before checking the condition.

Here's the basic syntax of a do-while loop:

```javascript
do {

// Code to be executed repeatedly

} while (condition);
```

For example, you can use a do-while loop to prompt a user for input until they enter a valid number:

```javascript
let userInput;

let number;

do {

userInput = prompt("Enter a number:");

number = parseInt(userInput);
```

```
} while (isNaN(number));
```

```
console.log(`You entered a valid number: ${number}`);
```

In this example: - The code inside the loop prompts the user for input and attempts to convert it to a number. - The loop continues to run as long as the condition isNaN(number) is true, meaning the user has not entered a valid number. Once a valid number is entered, the loop exits.

These are the three main types of loops in JavaScript, each serving different purposes. Understanding when and how to use them is crucial for controlling the flow of your programs and efficiently performing repetitive tasks. Loops are essential tools for processing arrays, iterating through objects, and managing program logic.

2.5 Functions and Scope

Functions are a fundamental concept in JavaScript, allowing you to encapsulate and reuse blocks of code. They also play a crucial role in defining variable scope within your programs. In this section, we'll explore functions, their syntax, and how scope works in JavaScript.

1. Function Declaration

A function is defined using the function keyword, followed by a name, a list of parameters enclosed in parentheses, and a block of code enclosed in curly braces. Here's the basic syntax:

```
function functionName(parameter1, parameter2, ...) {

// Code to be executed when the function is called

}
```

For example, let's create a simple function that adds two numbers:

```javascript
function addNumbers(a, b) {

return a + b;

}

const result = addNumbers(3, 5); // Calls the function and stores the
result in 'result'

console.log(result); // Outputs: 8
```

In this example, addNumbers is a function that takes two parameters (a and b) and returns their sum. When we call the function with addNumbers(3, 5), it returns 8, which is stored in the result variable.

2. Function Expression

Another way to define functions is through function expressions. In this approach, you assign a function to a variable. Here's the syntax:

```javascript
const functionName = function(parameter1, parameter2, ...) {

// Code to be executed when the function is called

};
```

Here's an example of a function expression that multiplies two numbers:

```javascript
const multiplyNumbers = function(x, y) {

return x * y;

};

const product = multiplyNumbers(4, 6);

console.log(product); // Outputs: 24
```

Function expressions are useful when you need to assign functions to variables, pass functions as arguments to other functions, or define functions dynamically.

3. Arrow Functions

Arrow functions provide a concise way to write functions in JavaScript. They are especially useful for small, one-line functions. The syntax looks like this:

const functionName = (parameter1, parameter2, ...) => {

// Code to be executed when the function is called

};

Here's an example of an arrow function that calculates the square of a number:

const square = (num) => num * num;

const squaredValue = square(5);

console.log(squaredValue); *// Outputs: 25*

Arrow functions have a more compact syntax and automatically capture the value of this from the surrounding context, making them popular for use in modern JavaScript code.

4. Function Scope

In JavaScript, variables declared within a function are scoped to that function. This means they are only accessible within the function. Variables declared outside of any function have global scope and can be accessed from anywhere in your code.

For example:

```javascript
function localScopeExample() {

const localVar = "I am local!";

console.log(localVar); // Outputs: I am local!

}

localScopeExample();

console.log(localVar); // Throws an error: localVar is not defined
```

In this example, localVar is defined within the localScopeExample function and cannot be accessed outside of it.

5. Function Parameters and Arguments

Parameters are placeholders for values that a function expects when it's called. Arguments are the actual values passed to a function when it's invoked.

For instance:

```javascript
function greet(name) {

console.log(`Hello, ${name}!`);

}

greet("Alice"); // "Alice" is the argument passed to the 'name' parameter
```

In this example, name is a parameter, and "Alice" is an argument.

6. Returning Values

Functions can return values using the return statement. When a function encounters a return statement, it exits immediately, and the specified value is returned to the caller.

```javascript
function subtract(a, b) {

return a - b;

}

const difference = subtract(10, 4);

console.log(difference); // Outputs: 6
```

In this example, the subtract function returns the result of a - b, which is 6.

Understanding functions and scope is crucial for organizing and reusing code effectively in JavaScript. Functions allow you to break down complex tasks into smaller, manageable parts and encapsulate logic. Scope defines where variables are accessible and helps prevent naming conflicts between different parts of your code. These concepts are fundamental for building maintainable and structured JavaScript applications.

Chapter 3: Working with DOM

3.1 Understanding the Document Object Model (DOM)

The Document Object Model (DOM) is a critical concept when working with web development, especially when using JavaScript to manipulate web pages dynamically. The DOM represents the structure and content of a web page as a tree-like structure of objects, allowing you to interact with and modify web page elements programmatically.

1. What Is the DOM?

The DOM is a programming interface for web documents. It represents the document as a tree of objects, where each object corresponds to a part of the web page, such as elements (e.g., headings, paragraphs, images), attributes, and text content. This tree-like structure is called the "DOM tree," and it provides a structured representation of the HTML content.

Here's a simple example of a DOM tree:

- Document (root)

- HTML

- Head

- Title

- Body

- H1

- P

- Image

In this tree, the Document object is the root of the DOM, and it contains HTML as its child, which, in turn, has Head and Body as its children, and so on. Each object in the tree corresponds to a specific element or part of the web page.

2. Why Is the DOM Important?

The DOM is crucial for web development because it enables you to:

- **Access and manipulate web page content:** You can use JavaScript to access and modify elements, attributes, and text content on a web page, making it interactive and dynamic.

- **Respond to user interactions:** With the DOM, you can create event listeners that respond to user actions like clicks, mouse movements, and keyboard inputs.

- **Dynamically update and change web page structure:** You can add, remove, or modify elements in real-time, allowing you to build dynamic web applications.

- **Retrieve and send data to a server:** JavaScript can use the DOM to access form data and send it to a server for processing.

3. How to Access the DOM

To access and interact with the DOM, you can use JavaScript. Here's how you typically access the DOM in a web page:

```
// Access the entire DOM tree (Document object)

const documentRoot = document;

// Access specific elements by their ID

const elementById = document.getElementById("elementId");

// Access elements by their tag name

const elementsByTagName = document.getElementsByTagName("tagname");

// Access elements by their class name

const elementsByClassName = document.getElementsByClassName("classname");

// Access elements using CSS selectors

const elementBySelector = document.querySelector("selector");

const elementsBySelectorAll = document.querySelectorAll("selector");
```

These methods allow you to access elements within the DOM tree based on their attributes, tags, or classes. Once you have a reference to an element, you can manipulate its properties and content using JavaScript.

4. Modifying the DOM

After accessing elements in the DOM, you can modify them in various ways. Common operations include:

- **Changing element content:** You can update text, HTML, or attributes of elements.

- **Adding or removing elements:** You can create new elements and append them to the DOM or remove existing ones.

- **Styling elements:** You can modify CSS properties to change the appearance of elements.

- **Handling events:** You can attach event listeners to elements to respond to user interactions.

Here's an example of changing the text content of an HTML element using JavaScript:

// Access an element by its ID

const element = document.getElementById("myElement");

// Change the text content of the element

element.textContent = "New text content";

In this example, we first access an element with the ID "myElement" and then change its text content using the textContent property.

Understanding the DOM is essential for web developers, as it forms the foundation for creating interactive and dynamic web applications. It enables you to access, manipulate, and update web page content, making it respond to user actions and behave dynamically. In the following sections, we'll delve deeper into DOM manipulation techniques, including selecting and manipulating elements, modifying their attributes, and handling events.

3.2 Selecting and Manipulating Elements

In web development, a common task is selecting HTML elements from the Document Object Model (DOM) and manipulating them using JavaScript. Understanding how to select and interact with elements is crucial for creating dynamic and interactive web pages. In this section, we'll explore different techniques for selecting elements and performing various manipulations.

1. Selecting Elements

By ID

You can select an element by its unique ID using the getElementById method:

```
const elementById = document.getElementById("elementId");
```

This method returns a reference to the element with the specified ID.

By Tag Name

To select elements by their tag name, you can use the getElementsByTagName method:

```
const elementsByTagName = document.getElementsByTagName("tagname");
```

This method returns a collection of elements with the given tag name, such as "div," "p," or "a."

By Class Name

Selecting elements by their class name is done using the getElementsByClassName method:

```
const elementsByClassName = document.getElementsByClassName("classname");
```

This method returns a collection of elements with the specified class name.

Using CSS Selectors

The querySelector and querySelectorAll methods allow you to select elements using CSS selectors:

```
const elementBySelector = document.querySelector("selector");
```

```
const elementsBySelectorAll = document.querySelectorAll("selector");
```

These methods are versatile and enable you to select elements based on complex CSS selector patterns.

2. Modifying Elements

Once you have selected elements, you can manipulate their content, attributes, and styles.

Changing Text Content

You can change the text content of an element using the textContent property:

```
const element = document.getElementById("myElement");
```

```
element.textContent = "New text content";
```

This updates the text displayed within the element.

Modifying HTML

To modify the HTML content of an element, you can use the innerHTML property:

```
const element = document.getElementById("myElement");
```

```
element.innerHTML = "<strong>Updated</strong> content";
```

This allows you to insert HTML markup into the element.

Changing Attributes

To modify element attributes, you can access them directly and assign new values:

```
const link = document.getElementById("myLink");
```

```
link.href = "https://example.com";
```

In this example, we update the href attribute of an anchor (<a>) element.

Styling Elements

You can change the style of elements by accessing their style property and modifying CSS properties:

```
const element = document.getElementById("myElement");
```

```
element.style.color = "blue";
```

element.style.fontSize = "16px";

This allows you to dynamically apply CSS styles to elements.

3. Adding and Removing Elements

Creating New Elements

To add new elements to the DOM, you can use the createElement method to create a new element, set its properties, and append it to an existing element:

const newDiv = document.createElement("div");

newDiv.textContent = "Newly created div";

document.body.appendChild(newDiv);

In this example, we create a new <div> element, set its text content, and append it to the <body> element.

Removing Elements

To remove an element from the DOM, you can use the remove method:

const   elementToRemove   =
document.getElementById("elementId");

elementToRemove.remove();

This code removes the specified element and its descendants from the DOM.

4. Event Handling

Event handling allows you to respond to user interactions with your web page. You can attach event listeners to elements, specifying which function to execute when an event occurs.

const button = document.getElementById("myButton");

button.addEventListener("click", **function**() {

alert("Button clicked!");

});

In this example, we add a click event listener to a button element, displaying an alert when the button is clicked.

Understanding how to select and manipulate elements in the DOM is foundational for web development. It enables you to create interactive and dynamic web pages by responding to user actions and dynamically updating content. These techniques are essential for building modern web applications and enhancing user experiences.

3.3 Modifying Element Content and Attributes

In web development, it's often necessary to dynamically modify the content and attributes of HTML elements in response to user interactions or other events. This section will cover how to change the content of elements, add, modify, and remove attributes, and explore the use of data attributes.

1. Changing Element Content

textContent and innerHTML

To change the text content of an HTML element, you can use the textContent property. For example:

```
const element = document.getElementById("myElement");

element.textContent = "New text content";
```

Alternatively, if you want to modify the HTML content within an element, you can use the innerHTML property:

```
const element = document.getElementById("myElement");

element.innerHTML = "<strong>Updated</strong> content";
```

Be cautious when using innerHTML with user-generated or untrusted content to avoid security vulnerabilities like cross-site scripting (XSS).

2. Modifying Element Attributes

Changing Attributes

You can change the attributes of an HTML element by accessing them and assigning new values. For example:

```
const link = document.getElementById("myLink");

link.href = "https://example.com";
```

In this example, we update the href attribute of an anchor (<a>) element.

Adding and Removing Attributes

To add attributes dynamically, you can use the setAttribute method:

const image = document.getElementById("myImage");

image.setAttribute("alt", "Alternative text");

This code adds or updates the alt attribute of an image element.

To remove an attribute, you can use the removeAttribute method:

const element = document.getElementById("myElement");

element.removeAttribute("attributeName");

Replace "attributeName" with the name of the attribute you want to remove.

3. Working with Data Attributes

HTML5 introduced the ability to define custom data attributes on HTML elements using the data- prefix. These attributes can store additional information related to an element and can be accessed and manipulated using JavaScript.

For example, you can define a data-id attribute on an element like this:

<**div id**="myDiv" **data-id**="123">Custom data attribute</**div**>

To access and modify this data attribute in JavaScript:

const element = document.getElementById("myDiv");

const dataId = element.getAttribute("data-id"); *// Get the value*

console.log(dataId); *// Outputs: "123"*

element.setAttribute("data-id", "456"); *// Set a new value*

Data attributes are a convenient way to associate data with elements and access it through JavaScript.

4. Adding and Removing Elements

Creating New Elements

To add new elements to the DOM, you can use the createElement method to create a new element, set its properties, and append it to an existing element:

const newDiv = document.createElement("div");

newDiv.textContent = "Newly created div";

document.body.appendChild(newDiv);

In this example, we create a new <div> element, set its text content, and append it to the <body> element.

Removing Elements

To remove an element from the DOM, you can use the remove method:

const elementToRemove = document.getElementById("elementId");

elementToRemove.remove();

This code removes the specified element and its descendants from the DOM.

In summary, understanding how to modify element content and attributes is fundamental in web development. These techniques allow you to create dynamic and interactive web pages by responding to user interactions and updating content dynamically. Properly handling element content and attributes is essential for building modern web applications and enhancing user experiences while maintaining security and performance best practices.

3.4 Event Handling in JavaScript

Event handling is a fundamental part of web development that allows you to create interactive and responsive web applications. With JavaScript, you can define event listeners to respond to various user actions and browser events, such as clicks, keyboard input, mouse movements, and more. In this section, we'll explore event handling in JavaScript.

1. Understanding Events

Events are occurrences or happenings in a web page that can trigger JavaScript code to execute. Examples of events include:

- Click: Triggered when a user clicks on an element.

- Mouseover and Mouseout: Fired when the mouse pointer enters or leaves an element.

- Keydown, Keypress, and Keyup: Events related to keyboard input.

- Submit: Fired when a form is submitted.

- Load: Triggered when a web page or an image finishes loading.

- Resize: Fired when the browser window is resized.

Events provide a way to make your web pages interactive by responding to user actions and other events.

2. Adding Event Listeners

To respond to events, you can add event listeners to HTML elements using JavaScript. An event listener is a JavaScript function that gets executed when a specified event occurs on an element. Here's the basic syntax for adding an event listener:

```
const element = document.getElementById("myElement");

element.addEventListener("eventName", eventHandlerFunction);
```

- element: The HTML element you want to attach the event listener to.

- "eventName": The name of the event you want to listen for (e.g., "click," "keydown").

- eventHandlerFunction: The JavaScript function that will be executed when the event occurs.

For example, to add a click event listener to a button element:

```
const button = document.getElementById("myButton");

button.addEventListener("click", function() {

alert("Button clicked!");

});
```

In this example, when the button with the ID "myButton" is clicked, an alert with the message "Button clicked!" will be displayed.

3. Event Object

When an event occurs, an event object is automatically created and passed to the event handler function as a parameter. This event object contains information about the event, such as the type of event, the target element that triggered the event, and more.

Here's an example of accessing the event object in an event handler function:

```javascript
const element = document.getElementById("myElement");

element.addEventListener("click", function(event) {

console.log(event.type); // Outputs: "click"

console.log(event.target); // Outputs the clicked element

});
```

You can use the event object to access information about the event and perform actions based on it.

4. Event Bubbling and Capturing

In JavaScript, events propagate through the DOM tree, and there are two phases: capturing and bubbling.

- **Capturing Phase:** Events are captured from the root of the DOM tree down to the target element.

- **Bubbling Phase:** Events are then bubbled up from the target element back to the root of the DOM tree.

You can specify whether you want to handle an event during the capturing or bubbling phase using the addEventListener method's third parameter, which is a boolean:

element.addEventListener("click",   eventHandlerFunction, useCapture);

- useCapture: A boolean value (default is false) that determines the phase in which the event is handled.

5. Removing Event Listeners

You can remove event listeners when they are no longer needed to prevent memory leaks and unexpected behavior. To remove an event listener, you need to specify the same event type and callback function used when adding the listener:

const element = document.getElementById("myElement");

function eventHandler() {

// Event handling logic

}

element.addEventListener("click", eventHandler);

// Later, to remove the event listener

element.removeEventListener("click", eventHandler);

Removing event listeners ensures that your code doesn't continue to respond to events after the relevant elements are no longer in use.

6. Event Delegation

Event delegation is a technique where you attach a single event listener to a parent element, which then handles events for its child elements. This is useful when you have multiple elements with the same behavior, like a list of items.

```javascript
const parentElement = document.getElementById("parentList");

parentElement.addEventListener("click", function(event) {

if (event.target.tagName === "LI") {

// Handle the click on an LI element

console.log("Item clicked:", event.target.textContent);

}

});
```

In this example, the click event is delegated from the parent element to its list items (<li>), allowing you to handle clicks on individual list items without attaching separate event listeners to each one.

Understanding event handling is essential for creating interactive web applications. It allows you to respond to user actions and make web pages dynamic. With event listeners, you can create responsive user interfaces and build web applications that provide a smooth and engaging user experience.

3.5 Working with Forms and User Input

Forms are an integral part of web applications, enabling users to input data and interact with websites. JavaScript plays a crucial role in enhancing form functionality and validating user input. In this section, we'll explore how to work with forms, access form elements, and handle user input using JavaScript.

1. Accessing Form Elements

To work with form elements in JavaScript, you can access them using various methods, such as getElementById, getElementsByName, or querySelector. For example, to access an input element with a specific id:

```javascript
const inputElement = document.getElementById("myInput");
```

You can also access elements by their name attribute:

```javascript
const radioButtons = document.getElementsByName("gender");
```

Once you have a reference to a form element, you can manipulate its properties, validate input, and respond to user interactions.

2. Form Submission

Forms are typically used to collect user data, and when a user submits a form, the data is sent to a server for processing. You can intercept the form submission using JavaScript to perform client-side validation or to prevent the default submission behavior.

```javascript
const form = document.getElementById("myForm");

form.addEventListener("submit", function(event) {

// Prevent the default form submission

event.preventDefault();

// Validate user input

const input = document.getElementById("myInput");

if (input.value === "") {

alert("Please fill out the field");

return;

}
```

```javascript
// Perform other actions or submit data to the server
```

```javascript
});
```

In this example, we prevent the default form submission behavior by calling event.preventDefault(). Then, we perform validation and take appropriate actions based on the user's input.

3. Input Validation

JavaScript is often used for client-side input validation to provide immediate feedback to users and improve the user experience. You can validate input by checking the values of form elements and displaying error messages if needed.

```javascript
const emailInput = document.getElementById("email");
```

```javascript
emailInput.addEventListener("blur", function() {
```

```javascript
const email = emailInput.value;
```

```javascript
if (!isValidEmail(email)) {
```

```javascript
alert("Invalid email address");
```

```javascript
}
```

```javascript
});
```

```javascript
function isValidEmail(email) {
```

```javascript
// Implement email validation logic
```

```javascript
// (e.g., using regular expressions)
```

```javascript
return /^[^\s@]+@[^\s@]+\.[^\s@]+$/.test(email);
```

```javascript
}
```

In this example, we add a blur event listener to an email input field to validate the email address when the user leaves the field. If the email is invalid, we display an alert message.

4. Working with Input Fields

JavaScript allows you to work with various types of form input fields, including text inputs, checkboxes, radio buttons, and dropdowns.

```javascript
const textInput = document.getElementById("textInput");

const checkbox = document.getElementById("checkbox");

const radioButton = document.querySelector('input[name="gender"]:checked');

const selectElement = document.getElementById("mySelect");

// Accessing input values

const textValue = textInput.value;

const isChecked = checkbox.checked;

const selectedValue = selectElement.value;
```

You can access and manipulate input values based on their types and properties.

5. Dynamic Form Elements

JavaScript enables you to dynamically modify form elements, such as adding or removing input fields based on user actions or application logic. This can provide a dynamic and user-friendly form experience.

```javascript
const addButton = document.getElementById("addButton");
```

```javascript
const formContainer = document.getElementById("formContainer");

addButton.addEventListener("click", function() {

const newInput = document.createElement("input");

newInput.type = "text";

formContainer.appendChild(newInput);

});
```

In this example, clicking a button adds a new text input field to the form dynamically.

6. Handling User Input Events

You can use various input events, such as change, input, focus, and blur, to respond to user input in real-time. These events allow you to perform actions as the user interacts with form elements.

```javascript
const inputElement = document.getElementById("myInput");

inputElement.addEventListener("input", function() {

// Perform actions as the user types

console.log("Input value changed:", inputElement.value);

});
```

By attaching event listeners to form elements, you can create dynamic and interactive forms that enhance the user experience and ensure data accuracy.

Understanding how to work with forms and user input is essential for building web applications that collect and process data efficiently.

JavaScript enables you to validate input, respond to user actions, and create dynamic forms that provide immediate feedback to users. Form handling is a crucial skill for web developers to create engaging and user-friendly web applications.

Chapter 4: JavaScript and HTML5

4.1 Canvas for Graphics and Animation

HTML5 introduced the <canvas> element, which provides a powerful way to draw graphics and create animations using JavaScript. With the HTML5 canvas, you can create interactive visual elements, such as charts, graphs, games, and dynamic illustrations, directly within a web page. In this section, we'll explore the basics of working with the HTML5 canvas element and how to draw graphics and animations using JavaScript.

1. The <canvas> Element

To use the <canvas> element, you need to include it in your HTML markup:

```html
<canvas id="myCanvas" width="400" height="200"></canvas>
```

- id: This attribute allows you to uniquely identify the canvas element.

- width and height: These attributes set the dimensions of the canvas in pixels.

2. Accessing the Canvas

In JavaScript, you can access the <canvas> element by its ID and obtain a drawing context, which is a JavaScript object that provides methods for drawing on the canvas:

```javascript
const canvas = document.getElementById("myCanvas");

const context = canvas.getContext("2d");
```

The getContext("2d") method returns a 2D rendering context, which is the most common and widely supported way to work with the canvas.

3. Drawing Shapes

You can draw various shapes on the canvas, including rectangles, circles, lines, and paths. Here's an example of drawing a simple rectangle:

// Draw a filled rectangle

context.fillStyle = "blue";

context.fillRect(50, 50, 100, 60);

In this code, we set the fill color to blue and draw a filled rectangle starting at coordinates (50, 50) with a width of 100 pixels and a height of 60 pixels.

4. Drawing Paths

Paths allow you to create custom shapes and complex drawings. You define a path by specifying a series of drawing commands, such as moveTo, lineTo, and arc, to create lines and curves. Here's an example of drawing a simple path:

// Draw a triangle

context.beginPath();

context.moveTo(150, 100); *// Move to the starting point*

context.lineTo(200, 50); *// Draw a line*

context.lineTo(250, 100); *// Draw another line*

context.closePath(); // *Close the path*

context.stroke(); // *Stroke the path outline*

In this code, we define a path to draw a triangle and then stroke it to create the outline.

5. Drawing Text

The canvas also allows you to render text on the screen. You can set the font, size, color, and alignment for text rendering:

context.font = "24px Arial";

context.fillStyle = "red";

context.textAlign = "center";

context.fillText("Hello, Canvas!", canvas.width / 2, canvas.height / 2);

In this example, we set the font, fill color, and text alignment and then use the fillText method to display text in the center of the canvas.

6. Animation

The HTML5 canvas is well-suited for creating animations. To create animations, you typically use the requestAnimationFrame function, which repeatedly calls a specified function to update the canvas content. Here's a basic example of animation:

function animate() {

// *Clear the canvas*

context.clearRect(0, 0, canvas.width, canvas.height);

```
// Update the animation state

// Draw objects or shapes

// Perform other animation logic

// Request the next animation frame

requestAnimationFrame(animate);

}

// Start the animation loop

animate();
```

In this code, the animate function is called repeatedly to update the canvas content. You can add your animation logic, such as moving objects, changing colors, or updating positions, within the animate function.

The HTML5 canvas is a powerful tool for creating dynamic and interactive graphics and animations on the web. By combining the canvas element with JavaScript, you can build games, data visualizations, and interactive web applications that engage users with visually appealing content. Understanding how to draw on the canvas and create animations is a valuable skill for web developers interested in visual design and user interaction.

4.2 Audio and Video Integration

HTML5 introduced native support for audio and video elements, making it easier than ever to include multimedia content in web pages without relying on third-party plugins like Flash. In this section, we'll explore how to integrate audio and video into web pages using the <audio> and <video> elements and JavaScript.

1. The <audio> Element

The <audio> element allows you to embed audio content directly in your web pages. You can specify the audio file's source using the src attribute, and users can play, pause, and control the audio playback.

<audio controls src="audio.mp3">

Your browser does not support the audio element.

</audio>

- controls: This attribute adds audio controls (play, pause, volume, etc.) to the player.

- src: Specifies the path to the audio file.

2. The <video> Element

The <video> element is similar to the <audio> element but is used for embedding video content. You can specify multiple video sources to ensure compatibility with various browsers and devices.

<video controls>

<source src="video.mp4" type="video/mp4">

<source src="video.webm" type="video/webm">

Your browser does not support the video element.

</video>

In this example, we provide two video sources in different formats, "mp4" and "webm," to ensure cross-browser compatibility.

3. Controlling Playback with JavaScript

JavaScript enables you to programmatically control audio and video playback. You can access the <audio> and <video> elements using the DOM and call their methods and properties.

```javascript
const audioElement = document.getElementById("myAudio");

const videoElement = document.getElementById("myVideo");

// Play audio and video

audioElement.play();

videoElement.play();

// Pause audio and video

audioElement.pause();

videoElement.pause();

// Adjust volume (0 to 1)

audioElement.volume = 0.5;

videoElement.volume = 0.7;

// Get current playback time (in seconds)

const currentTime = audioElement.currentTime;

// Set the current playback time (jump to a specific position)

audioElement.currentTime = 30; // Jump to 30 seconds
```

Using JavaScript, you can create custom controls for audio and video players, implement playback logic, and respond to user interactions.

4. Events and Callbacks

Both <audio> and <video> elements fire a variety of events during playback, such as "play," "pause," "ended," and "timeupdate." You can use event listeners to respond to these events.

```javascript
audioElement.addEventListener("play", function() {

console.log("Audio playback started");

});

videoElement.addEventListener("ended", function() {

console.log("Video playback ended");

});
```

This code listens for the "play" event on an audio element and the "ended" event on a video element and logs messages when these events occur.

5. Media APIs

HTML5 provides JavaScript APIs for working with audio and video elements more extensively. The Web Audio API, for example, allows for real-time audio processing, creating audio visualizations, and more advanced audio manipulation. Similarly, the MediaStream API allows access to device cameras and microphones for video conferencing and multimedia applications.

```javascript
// Example using the Web Audio API

const audioContext = new (window.AudioContext || window.webkitAudioContext)();
```

```javascript
const audioSource = audioContext.createMediaElementSource(audioElement);

const analyser = audioContext.createAnalyser();

// Connect the audio source to the analyser and speakers

audioSource.connect(analyser);

analyser.connect(audioContext.destination);

// Analyze audio data (e.g., for creating visualizations)

analyser.fftSize = 256;

const bufferLength = analyser.frequencyBinCount;

const dataArray = new Uint8Array(bufferLength);

analyser.getByteFrequencyData(dataArray);
```

These APIs provide advanced capabilities for audio and video processing, enabling the creation of multimedia applications with interactive and real-time features.

6. Accessibility and Compatibility

When integrating audio and video into web pages, it's essential to consider accessibility and compatibility. Provide alternative text and captions for multimedia content to ensure it is accessible to users with disabilities. Additionally, use formats that are widely supported across browsers and platforms.

HTML5's native support for audio and video has made it much simpler to include multimedia content in web applications. By understanding how to use the <audio> and <video> elements, control playback with JavaScript, respond to events, and leverage advanced media APIs, you can create engaging and interactive multimedia experiences for your web users while ensuring accessibility and compatibility.

4.3 Geolocation and Maps

Geolocation is a feature that allows web applications to determine a user's geographical location. It can be incredibly useful for a variety of applications, from providing location-based services to tracking delivery orders. In addition to geolocation, integrating maps into web applications has become increasingly popular. In this section, we'll explore geolocation and how to integrate maps using JavaScript.

1. Geolocation API

The Geolocation API provides a straightforward way to access a user's location using JavaScript. You can use the navigator.geolocation object to obtain the user's latitude and longitude coordinates.

```javascript
if ("geolocation" in navigator) {

navigator.geolocation.getCurrentPosition(function(position) {

const latitude = position.coords.latitude;

const longitude = position.coords.longitude;

console.log(`Latitude: ${latitude}, Longitude: ${longitude}`);

});

} else {

console.log("Geolocation is not supported by this browser.");
```

```
}
```

In this code, we first check if the browser supports geolocation using "geolocation" in navigator. If supported, we use getCurrentPosition to retrieve the user's coordinates, and then we can access the latitude and longitude.

2. Handling Geolocation Errors

When using the Geolocation API, it's essential to handle errors gracefully. Users may deny access to their location, or there may be other issues preventing location retrieval.

```
navigator.geolocation.getCurrentPosition(

function(position) {

// Handle successful location retrieval

},

function(error) {

switch (error.code) {

case error.PERMISSION_DENIED:

console.log("User denied geolocation request.");

break;

case error.POSITION_UNAVAILABLE:

console.log("Location information is unavailable.");

break;

case error.TIMEOUT:
```

```
console.log("Request to get user location timed out.");

break;

default:

console.log("An unknown error occurred.");

break;

}

}

);
```

In this code, we pass a second callback function to getCurrentPosition to handle errors. We check the error.code to determine the specific error that occurred.

3. Integrating Maps with JavaScript

Integrating maps into web applications is commonly done using third-party mapping libraries such as Google Maps, Mapbox, or Leaflet. These libraries provide APIs that allow you to embed maps, add markers, and create interactive map-based experiences.

Here's a basic example using the Google Maps JavaScript API:

```
<!DOCTYPE html>

<html>

<head>

<script src="https://maps.googleapis.com/maps/api/js?key=YOUR_API_KEY&libraries=places"></script>
```

```html
</head>
<body>
<div id="map" style="width: 100%; height: 400px;"></div>
<script>
function initMap() {
const map = new google.maps.Map(document.getElementById("map"), {
center: { lat: -34.397, lng: 150.644 },
zoom: 8,
});

const marker = new google.maps.Marker({
position: { lat: -34.397, lng: 150.644 },
map: map,
title: "Marker Title",
});
}
</script>
<script async defer
src="https://maps.googleapis.com/maps/api/
js?key=YOUR_API_KEY&callback=initMap">
</script>
```

```
</body>

</html>
```

In this example, replace YOUR_API_KEY with your Google Maps API key. The code initializes a map and adds a marker to it.

4. Map Libraries and APIs

There are various map libraries and APIs available for creating interactive maps. Some popular ones include:

- Google Maps JavaScript API: Provides extensive features for embedding Google Maps into web applications.

- Mapbox: Offers customizable maps, geocoding, and location search services.

- Leaflet: A lightweight and open-source JavaScript library for interactive maps.

Each library or API has its unique features and capabilities, so you can choose the one that best suits your project's requirements.

5. Geolocation in Real-World Applications

Geolocation and maps are used in various real-world applications, such as:

- Location-based services: Apps that provide nearby restaurant recommendations, weather updates, or local event information.

- Ride-sharing and navigation: Services like Uber and Lyft rely on real-time location data.

- Delivery tracking: Companies like Amazon use geolocation to track the delivery status of packages.

- Social networking: Apps like Instagram allow users to tag their posts with location information.

By leveraging geolocation and maps in your web applications, you can enhance user experiences and provide valuable location-based features.

6. Privacy Considerations

When using geolocation, it's essential to consider user privacy. Always ask for user consent before accessing their location. Additionally, be transparent about how the collected location data will be used and provide options for users to control their privacy settings.

Geolocation and maps have opened up a wide range of possibilities for web applications. Whether you need to provide location-based services, create interactive maps, or simply display a user's current location, understanding geolocation and map integration is a valuable skill for web developers.

4.4 Local Storage and Web Storage

Local storage and web storage are client-side storage solutions that allow web applications to store data directly in the user's browser. This data can be used to persist user preferences, cache application data, or provide offline functionality. In this section, we'll explore local storage and web storage in JavaScript and how they can be utilized in web development.

1. Local Storage vs. Web Storage

Local storage and web storage are mechanisms for storing key-value pairs in the browser, but they differ in terms of scope and capacity:

- **Local Storage** (localStorage): Data stored in local storage is persistent across browser sessions and can be accessed across different tabs or windows of the same browser. It has a larger storage capacity compared to web storage (usually around 5-10 MB per domain). Local storage data is not sent to the server with every HTTP request, making it suitable for caching and storing user settings.

- **Session Storage** (sessionStorage): Data stored in session storage is only available for the duration of a single page session. It is limited to the lifetime of the page and is not shared between different tabs or windows. Session storage is useful for temporary data storage during a user's interaction with a web page.

2. Storing Data

You can store data in local storage or session storage using the setItem method by providing a key-value pair:

// Storing data in local storage

```
localStorage.setItem("username", "john_doe");
```

// Storing data in session storage

```
sessionStorage.setItem("theme", "dark");
```

In this example, we store a username in local storage and a theme preference in session storage.

3. Retrieving Data

To retrieve data from local storage or session storage, you can use the getItem method with the corresponding key:

```
// Retrieving data from local storage

const username = localStorage.getItem("username");

// Retrieving data from session storage

const theme = sessionStorage.getItem("theme");
```

The getItem method returns the stored value associated with the provided key.

4. Removing Data

You can remove data from local storage or session storage using the removeItem method:

```
// Removing data from local storage

localStorage.removeItem("username");

// Removing data from session storage

sessionStorage.removeItem("theme");
```

This removes the key-value pair associated with the specified key.

5. Clearing Storage

If you need to remove all data stored in local storage or session storage, you can use the clear method:

// Clearing local storage

localStorage.clear();

// Clearing session storage

sessionStorage.clear();

Be cautious when clearing storage, as it will remove all data stored in the respective storage area.

6. Storage Events

Both local storage and session storage emit storage events when their data is modified by scripts from other windows or tabs of the same origin. You can listen for these events to react to changes made by other parts of your application:

```javascript
window.addEventListener("storage", function(event) {

console.log(`Storage event: ${event.key} was changed from ${event.oldValue} to ${event.newValue}`);

});
```

This event handler will be called whenever data is modified in local storage or session storage by other scripts within the same origin.

7. Limitations and Considerations

- Data stored in local storage and session storage is limited to strings. You can serialize complex data structures like objects into JSON strings before storing them and deserialize them when retrieving.

• Both storage mechanisms are synchronous, meaning that reading and writing data can block the main thread. Be mindful of performance considerations, especially when dealing with large amounts of data.

• Storage space is limited (around 5-10 MB for local storage), so avoid storing excessive data or sensitive information in client-side storage.

• Browser support for local storage and session storage is nearly universal, making them reliable choices for web application development.

Local storage and web storage provide a convenient way to store and manage data on the client side, reducing the need for constant server requests and improving user experience. Understanding how to use local storage and session storage effectively is valuable for web developers looking to enhance their web applications with data persistence and caching capabilities.

4.5 Web Workers for Multithreading

Web Workers are a feature of modern web browsers that enable multithreading in web applications. They allow JavaScript code to run concurrently in the background, separate from the main thread, which is responsible for handling the user interface and rendering. This can significantly improve the performance and responsiveness of web applications, especially for tasks that involve heavy computation, data processing, or long-running operations. In this section, we'll explore Web Workers and how to use them in web development.

1. Creating a Web Worker

To create a Web Worker, you need to create a separate JavaScript file dedicated to the worker's task. Let's say we want to perform a time-consuming calculation in a Web Worker. Here's how you create the worker file, calculation.js:

```javascript
// calculation.js

self.addEventListener("message", function(e) {

const data = e.data;

// Perform the time-consuming calculation

const result = performCalculation(data);

// Send the result back to the main thread

self.postMessage(result);

});

function performCalculation(data) {

// Perform the calculation here

return data * 2;

}
```

In this example, we define an event listener that listens for messages from the main thread. When a message is received, it triggers the performCalculation function and sends the result back to the main thread using self.postMessage.

2. Using a Web Worker in the Main Thread

To use the Web Worker in the main thread, you need to create an instance of it and send and receive messages. Here's how you can do it:

```javascript
// main.js

// Create a new Web Worker instance

const worker = new Worker("calculation.js");

// Send data to the worker

const inputData = 5;

worker.postMessage(inputData);

// Receive the result from the worker

worker.addEventListener("message", function(e) {

const result = e.data;

console.log(`Result from Web Worker: ${result}`);

});
```

In this code, we create a new Web Worker instance by providing the path to the worker script. We send data to the worker using postMessage and listen for messages from the worker using an event listener.

3. Benefits of Web Workers

- **Improved Responsiveness**: Web Workers prevent long-running tasks from blocking the main thread, ensuring that your web application remains responsive to user interactions.

• **Parallel Processing**: You can utilize multiple Web Workers to perform parallel processing, taking advantage of multi-core processors and speeding up tasks like data processing and image manipulation.

• **Offloading Heavy Tasks**: Tasks such as image filtering, encryption, or complex calculations can be offloaded to Web Workers, reducing the workload on the main thread and preventing slowdowns.

4. Limitations and Considerations

• **No DOM Access**: Web Workers do not have access to the DOM or the global window object. They are meant for pure computation tasks and cannot directly manipulate the DOM or interact with the user interface.

• **Communication Overhead**: Data sent between the main thread and Web Workers is serialized and deserialized, which can introduce some communication overhead. Avoid sending large data objects between threads.

• **Same-Origin Policy**: Web Workers follow the same-origin policy, meaning they can only communicate with the same domain they were loaded from. This policy is essential for security reasons.

• **Resource Duplication**: Each Web Worker instance has its own global scope and cannot directly share variables or data with other workers. If necessary, you can use techniques like shared memory or libraries designed for inter-worker communication.

Web Workers are a valuable tool for improving web application performance and responsiveness, especially for CPU-intensive tasks. By utilizing the power of multithreading, you can enhance the user experience and ensure that your web application remains smooth and responsive even when handling computationally intensive operations.

Chapter 5: Advanced JavaScript Concepts

5.1 Closures and Lexical Scoping

Closures and lexical scoping are fundamental concepts in JavaScript that play a crucial role in its functional nature and the management of variable scope. Understanding closures and lexical scoping is essential for writing clean and maintainable JavaScript code.

1. Lexical Scoping

Lexical scoping, also known as static scoping, defines how variable names are resolved in nested functions. In JavaScript, variables are scoped based on their location within the source code, and this scope is determined at compile time. This means that a variable's scope is defined by its surrounding function or block of code.

```javascript
function outer() {

const outerVar = "I'm in the outer function";

function inner() {

const innerVar = "I'm in the inner function";

console.log(outerVar); // Accessing outerVar from inner function

}

inner();

}

outer();
```

In this example, the inner function has access to variables declared in its containing function, outer, due to lexical scoping. It can access outerVar because it's within the lexical scope of outer.

2. Closures

A closure is a function that "closes over" its lexical scope, allowing it to access variables from its containing function even after the containing function has finished executing. Closures are created whenever a function is defined within another function.

```javascript
function createCounter() {

let count = 0;

return function () {

count++;

console.log(count);

};

}

const counter = createCounter();

counter(); // Outputs 1

counter(); // Outputs 2
```

In this example, createCounter returns an inner function that maintains access to the count variable even after createCounter has completed execution. This is the essence of a closure.

3. Practical Uses of Closures

Closures are widely used in JavaScript for various purposes:

- **Data Encapsulation**: Closures can be used to encapsulate data and expose only the necessary parts, providing a way to implement private variables.

```javascript
function createPerson(name) {

let age = 0;

return {

getName: function () {

return name;

},

getAge: function () {

return age;

},

setAge: function (newAge) {

if (newAge >= 0) {

age = newAge;

}

},

};

}

const person = createPerson("Alice");

console.log(person.getName()); // Outputs "Alice"
```

```javascript
person.setAge(30);

console.log(person.getAge()); // Outputs 30
```

- **Function Factories**: Closures enable the creation of function factories, where you generate functions with different behaviors based on input parameters.

```javascript
function createMultiplier(factor) {

return function (number) {

return number * factor;

};

}

const double = createMultiplier(2);

console.log(double(5)); // Outputs 10

const triple = createMultiplier(3);

console.log(triple(5)); // Outputs 15
```

- **Callback Functions**: Closures are frequently used in callback functions to maintain context and access variables from the enclosing scope.

```javascript
function fetchData(url, callback) {

fetch(url)

.then((response) => response.json())

.then((data) => callback(data))
```

```javascript
.catch((error) => console.error(error));

}

const apiUrl = "https://api.example.com/data";

fetchData(apiUrl, function (data) {

console.log(data);

});
```

Understanding closures and lexical scoping is essential for mastering JavaScript. These concepts empower developers to write clean and efficient code by controlling variable scope, creating reusable functions, and encapsulating data effectively. Closures, in particular, play a crucial role in many advanced JavaScript patterns and functional programming techniques.

ASSISTANT

Chapter 5: Advanced JavaScript Concepts

5.1 Closures and Lexical Scoping

Closures and lexical scoping are advanced JavaScript concepts that play a crucial role in the language's flexibility and power. They involve the scope in which functions are declared and the ability of functions to "remember" their lexical scope even when executed elsewhere. Understanding closures and lexical scoping is essential for writing efficient and maintainable JavaScript code.

1. Lexical Scoping

Lexical scoping, also known as static scoping, determines the scope of a variable by its position within the source code. In JavaScript, variables declared with var, let, or const have lexical scope. This means that the scope of a variable is determined by its location in the source code when the code is written, not when it's executed.

```javascript
function outer() {

const message = "Hello, ";

function inner(name) {

console.log(message + name);

}

return inner;

}

const greet = outer();
```

greet("Alice"); // *Output: Hello, Alice*

In this example, the inner function has access to the message variable from its outer scope, demonstrating lexical scoping.

2. Closures

A closure is a function bundled together with the variables from its surrounding lexical scope. It allows a function to "remember" and access variables from its parent scope, even after the parent function has finished executing.

```javascript
function counter() {

let count = 0;

return function() {

count++;

console.log(count);

};

}

const increment = counter();

increment(); // Output: 1

increment(); // Output: 2
```

In this code, the increment function forms a closure over the count variable, retaining access to it between calls.

3. Practical Use Cases

Closures and lexical scoping are fundamental in JavaScript and have practical applications, such as:

- **Data Encapsulation**: Closures allow you to encapsulate data and behavior within functions, creating private variables and methods that are not accessible from outside the function.

- **Module Pattern**: Closures are often used to implement the module pattern, where functions and variables are scoped within a closure to create reusable and isolated modules.

- **Callbacks**: Closures are commonly used in callbacks, allowing functions to "remember" their context and access variables from their parent scope even when invoked later.

- **Asynchronous Programming**: Closures are essential in dealing with asynchronous code. They help maintain the state and context in callback functions, promises, and async/await.

4. Memory Management

While closures are powerful, they can also lead to memory-related issues if not managed correctly. When a function forms a closure over variables from its parent scope, those variables are retained in memory as long as the closure exists. This can result in memory leaks if closures are not released when they are no longer needed.

To mitigate memory issues, be mindful of closures in long-running applications, and consider techniques like event unbinding and object disposal to release closures and their associated memory.

5. Lexical Scoping in Arrow Functions

Arrow functions in JavaScript have lexical scoping behavior that differs slightly from regular functions. They inherit their lexical scope from their surrounding code block, which means they don't create their own this, arguments, or super bindings. This can be both advantageous and challenging, depending on the context in which arrow functions are used.

```javascript
function regularFunction() {

return () => {

console.log(this); // Lexical 'this' from regularFunction

};

}

const arrowFunc = regularFunction();

arrowFunc(); // Output: regularFunction's 'this'
```

In this example, the arrow function inherits the this value from its parent scope, which is the regularFunction. This behavior can be useful for maintaining context in callback functions.

6. Conclusion

Closures and lexical scoping are powerful concepts in JavaScript that enable advanced programming techniques and patterns. By understanding how lexical scope works, how closures are formed, and their practical applications, you can write more maintainable and expressive JavaScript code. However, be cautious with memory management when dealing with long-lived closures to avoid potential memory leaks in your applications.

5.2 Object-Oriented Programming in JavaScript

Object-oriented programming (OOP) is a fundamental programming paradigm that emphasizes the use of objects and classes for organizing and structuring code. JavaScript is a versatile language that supports both classical and prototypal inheritance, making it a powerful choice for OOP. In this section, we'll explore the principles of object-oriented programming in JavaScript and how to create and work with objects and classes.

1. Objects in JavaScript

In JavaScript, objects are collections of key-value pairs, where keys are strings (or Symbols) and values can be any data type, including other objects. Objects are at the core of JavaScript, and they can be created in various ways:

```javascript
// Creating an object using object literal syntax

const person = {

firstName: "John",

lastName: "Doe",

age: 30,

};

// Creating an object using the Object constructor
```

```javascript
const car = new Object();

car.make = "Toyota";

car.model = "Camry";

car.year = 2022;
```

You can access object properties using dot notation (person.firstName) or bracket notation (person["firstName"]).

2. Prototypal Inheritance

JavaScript uses a prototypal inheritance model, where objects can inherit properties and methods from other objects. Every object in JavaScript has an associated prototype object, and this chain of prototypes forms the basis of inheritance.

```javascript
// Creating a prototype object

const vehiclePrototype = {

startEngine() {

console.log("Engine started.");

},

};

// Creating an object that inherits from the prototype

const car = Object.create(vehiclePrototype);

car.make = "Toyota";

car.model = "Camry";

car.startEngine(); // Output: Engine started.
```

In this example, the car object inherits the startEngine method from its prototype, vehiclePrototype.

3. Constructor Functions

Constructor functions are used to create multiple objects with similar properties and methods. They are conventionally named with an initial capital letter and are invoked using the new keyword.

// Constructor function for creating person objects

function Person(firstName, lastName, age) {

this.firstName = firstName;

this.lastName = lastName;

this.age = age;

}

// Creating person objects using the constructor

const person1 = **new** Person("Alice", "Johnson", 25);

const person2 = **new** Person("Bob", "Smith", 30);

Constructor functions can be thought of as blueprints for creating objects, and the this keyword refers to the new object being created.

4. Classes in ES6

ES6 introduced the class syntax, which provides a more structured way to define constructor functions and manage prototypes. Classes are a syntactical sugar over constructor functions and prototypes, making OOP in JavaScript more intuitive.

// Defining a class for creating person objects

```javascript
class Person {

constructor(firstName, lastName, age) {

this.firstName = firstName;

this.lastName = lastName;

this.age = age;

}

}

// Creating person objects using the class

const person1 = new Person("Alice", "Johnson", 25);

const person2 = new Person("Bob", "Smith", 30);
```

Classes can also define methods within their bodies, making it easier to encapsulate behavior related to the class.

5. Inheritance with Classes

ES6 classes support inheritance through the extends keyword. You can create subclasses that inherit properties and methods from a parent class.

```javascript
// Parent class

class Vehicle {

constructor(make, model) {

this.make = make;

this.model = model;
```

```javascript
}

startEngine() {

console.log("Engine started.");

}

}

// Subclass

class Car extends Vehicle {

constructor(make, model, year) {

super(make, model);

this.year = year;

}

}

const car = new Car("Toyota", "Camry", 2022);

car.startEngine(); // Output: Engine started.
```

In this example, the Car class inherits from the Vehicle class and extends its behavior.

6. Encapsulation and Abstraction

OOP principles such as encapsulation and abstraction allow you to create clean and maintainable code. Encapsulation involves bundling data (properties) and methods (functions) together within an object, providing control over their accessibility. Abstraction focuses on hiding complex implementation details and exposing a simplified interface.

7. Polymorphism and Inheritance

Polymorphism allows objects of different classes to be treated as objects of a common superclass. In JavaScript, polymorphism is achieved through method overriding and dynamic method binding.

```
class Animal {

speak() {

console.log("Animal makes a sound.");

}

}

class Dog extends Animal {

speak() {

console.log("Dog barks.");

}

}

const animal = new Animal();

const dog = new Dog();

animal.speak(); // Output: Animal makes a sound.

dog.speak(); // Output: Dog barks.
```

In this example, both animal and dog are treated as Animal objects, but their speak methods behave differently.

8. Conclusion

Object-oriented programming is a powerful paradigm for structuring and organizing code, and JavaScript provides the flexibility to implement OOP principles using both prototypes and classes. Understanding how to create and manipulate objects, use inheritance, and apply OOP concepts will help you write more modular, maintainable, and expressive JavaScript code for complex applications.

5.3 Prototypes and Inheritance

Prototypes and inheritance are fundamental concepts in JavaScript that allow objects to share properties and methods with other objects. Understanding prototypes is crucial for creating efficient and maintainable code when working with objects. In this section, we'll delve into prototypes, how they relate to inheritance, and how they can be used in JavaScript.

1. Prototypes in JavaScript

In JavaScript, every object has a prototype. A prototype is an object from which other objects inherit properties and methods. The prototype relationship forms a chain, commonly referred to as the prototype chain.

```javascript
// Creating an object

const person = {

firstName: "John",

lastName: "Doe",

};
```

// Accessing properties using the prototype chain

console.log(person.firstName); *// Output: John*

console.log(person.hasOwnProperty("firstName")); *// Output: true*

In this example, the person object inherits properties and methods from its prototype, which is the built-in Object prototype.

2. The Prototype Chain

The prototype chain allows objects to delegate property and method access to their prototypes. When you try to access a property or method on an object, JavaScript first checks if the object has that property or method. If it doesn't, JavaScript looks up the prototype chain until it finds the property or method or reaches the end of the chain.

// Creating a prototype object

const vehiclePrototype = {

startEngine() {

console.log("Engine started.");

},

};

// Creating an object that inherits from the prototype

const car = Object.create(vehiclePrototype);

// Accessing a method through the prototype chain

car.startEngine(); *// Output: Engine started.*

In this example, the car object inherits the startEngine method from its prototype, vehiclePrototype.

3. Constructor Functions and Prototypes

Constructor functions are often used to create objects that share the same properties and methods. When you create objects using a constructor function, they automatically have a prototype object associated with them.

```
// Constructor function

function Person(firstName, lastName) {

this.firstName = firstName;

this.lastName = lastName;

}

// Creating objects using the constructor

const person1 = new Person("Alice", "Johnson");

const person2 = new Person("Bob", "Smith");

console.log(person1.firstName); // Output: Alice

console.log(person2.lastName); // Output: Smith
```

In this example, person1 and person2 are instances of the Person constructor, and they share a prototype.

4. Adding Properties and Methods to Prototypes

You can add properties and methods to an object's prototype, making them available to all instances of that object.

```javascript
// Constructor function

function Person(firstName, lastName) {

this.firstName = firstName;

this.lastName = lastName;

}

// Adding a method to the prototype

Person.prototype.getFullName = function() {

return this.firstName + " " + this.lastName;

};

const person1 = new Person("Alice", "Johnson");

const person2 = new Person("Bob", "Smith");

console.log(person1.getFullName()); // Output: Alice Johnson

console.log(person2.getFullName()); // Output: Bob Smith
```

In this example, the getFullName method is added to the Person constructor's prototype, allowing all instances of Person to access it.

5. Inheritance through Prototypes

Prototypes enable inheritance in JavaScript. You can create object hierarchies where objects inherit properties and methods from other objects in the prototype chain.

```javascript
// Parent constructor function

function Animal(name) {
```

```javascript
this.name = name;

}

// Adding a method to the parent prototype

Animal.prototype.makeSound = function() {

console.log("Animal makes a sound.");

};

// Child constructor function

function Dog(name) {

Animal.call(this, name); // Call the parent constructor

}

// Inheriting from the parent prototype

Dog.prototype = Object.create(Animal.prototype);

Dog.prototype.constructor = Dog;

// Adding a method to the child prototype

Dog.prototype.bark = function() {

console.log("Dog barks.");

};

const dog = new Dog("Rex");

dog.makeSound(); // Output: Animal makes a sound.

dog.bark(); // Output: Dog barks.
```

In this example, the Dog constructor inherits properties and methods from the Animal constructor through their prototypes.

6. ES6 Classes and Inheritance

ES6 introduced a more structured way to work with prototypes and inheritance through the class syntax.

```javascript
// Parent class

class Animal {

constructor(name) {

this.name = name;

}

makeSound() {

console.log("Animal makes a sound.");

}

}

// Child class

class Dog extends Animal {

constructor(name) {

super(name); // Call the parent constructor

}

bark() {

console.log("Dog barks.");
```

```javascript
  }
}

const dog = new Dog("Rex");

dog.makeSound(); // Output: Animal makes a sound.

dog.bark(); // Output: Dog barks.
```

ES6 classes provide a more concise and intuitive way to create and extend classes in JavaScript while still utilizing the prototype chain for inheritance.

7. Conclusion

Prototypes and inheritance are core concepts in JavaScript that enable code reusability and hierarchy in object-oriented programming. Understanding how prototypes work, how to add properties and methods to them, and how to create object hierarchies is essential for writing efficient and maintainable JavaScript code. Whether you choose to use constructor functions and prototypes or ES6 classes, these concepts form the foundation of object-oriented programming in JavaScript.

5.4 Promises and Asynchronous Programming

Promises are a critical feature in JavaScript for handling asynchronous operations. They provide a cleaner and more structured way to work with asynchronous code compared to traditional callback functions. In this section, we'll explore promises, how they work, and how they enable asynchronous programming in JavaScript.

1. Understanding Asynchronous JavaScript

Asynchronous operations are tasks that don't block the main execution thread of a program. Common examples include making HTTP requests, reading files, and waiting for user interactions. JavaScript is single-threaded, which means it can only execute one operation at a time. However, it can simulate concurrency by leveraging asynchronous programming techniques.

```javascript
// Example of an asynchronous operation

setTimeout(function() {

console.log("Async operation completed.");

}, 1000);

console.log("Main thread continues.");
```

In this code, the setTimeout function schedules an asynchronous task to run after 1000 milliseconds. While waiting for the task to complete, the main thread continues executing other code.

2. Callbacks and Callback Hell

Callbacks have traditionally been used to manage asynchronous operations in JavaScript. A callback is a function that's passed as an argument to another function and executed when the operation is complete.

```javascript
function fetchData(callback) {

setTimeout(function() {

const data = { message: "Data fetched." };

callback(data);
```

```
}, 1000);

}

fetchData(function(result) {

console.log(result.message);

});
```

However, as applications grow and involve multiple asynchronous operations, nested callbacks can lead to a phenomenon known as "callback hell" or "pyramid of doom." This makes the code hard to read and maintain.

3. Introducing Promises

Promises were introduced to address the callback hell problem and provide a more structured way to work with asynchronous code. A promise represents a value that might not be available yet but will be in the future. Promises have three states: pending, resolved (fulfilled), and rejected.

```
// Creating a promise

const fetchData = new Promise(function(resolve, reject) {

setTimeout(function() {

const data = { message: "Data fetched." };

resolve(data); // Resolve the promise with data

}, 1000);

});

// Using the promise
```

```
fetchData

.then(function(result) {

console.log(result.message);

})

.catch(function(error) {

console.error(error);

});
```

In this example, the fetchData promise represents an asynchronous operation. It can be resolved with data or rejected with an error. The then method is used to handle the resolved state, while the catch method handles rejections.

4. Chaining Promises

One of the advantages of promises is the ability to chain multiple asynchronous operations in a more readable and maintainable way.

```
function fetchData() {

return new Promise(function(resolve, reject) {

setTimeout(function() {

const data = { message: "Data fetched." };

resolve(data);

}, 1000);

});

}
```

```javascript
function processData(data) {

return new Promise(function(resolve, reject) {

setTimeout(function() {

data.processed = true;

resolve(data);

}, 1000);

});

}

fetchData()

.then(processData)

.then(function(result) {

console.log(result.message); // Output: Data fetched.

console.log(result.processed); // Output: true

})

.catch(function(error) {

console.error(error);

});
```

In this example, the fetchData and processData functions return promises, allowing them to be chained together. This results in a more linear and readable flow of asynchronous operations.

5. Promise.all and Promise.race

The Promise.all method is used when you have multiple promises that need to be resolved before proceeding.

```javascript
const promise1 = fetchData();

const promise2 = processData();

Promise.all([promise1, promise2])

.then(function(results) {

console.log(results[0].message); // Output: Data fetched.

console.log(results[1].processed); // Output: true

})

.catch(function(error) {

console.error(error);

});
```

Promise.all waits for all promises in the array to be resolved before calling the .then handler.

On the other hand, Promise.race is used when you want to execute a task as soon as the first promise in an array resolves or rejects.

```javascript
const promise1 = fetchData();

const promise2 = new Promise(function(resolve, reject) {

setTimeout(function() {

reject(new Error("Promise 2 rejected."));
```

```javascript
}, 500);

});

Promise.race([promise1, promise2])

.then(function(result) {

console.log(result.message); // Output: Data fetched.

})

.catch(function(error) {

console.error(error); // Output: Error: Promise 2 rejected.

});
```

Promise.race resolves or rejects as soon as any of the promises in the array does.

6. Async/Await

ES6 introduced the async and await keywords, which simplify working with promises even further. The async keyword is used to declare an asynchronous function, while await is used within an async function to pause execution until a promise is resolved.

```javascript
async function fetchData() {

return new Promise(function(resolve) {

setTimeout(function() {

const data = { message: "Data fetched." };

resolve(data);

}, 1000);
```

```javascript
});

}

async function processAsyncData() {

const data = await fetchData();

console.log(data.message); // Output: Data fetched.
```

##

5.5 Error Handling and Debugging

Error handling and debugging are essential skills **for** any JavaScript developer. As your code becomes more complex, it's crucial to identify and resolve errors efficiently. In this section, we'll explore various error-handling techniques and debugging tools to help you troubleshoot issues **in** your JavaScript code.

1. Understanding JavaScript Errors

JavaScript code can encounter various types **of** errors, including syntax errors, runtime errors, and logical errors.

- **Syntax Errors:** These occur when your code violates the language's syntax rules. They are detected by the JavaScript engine during parsing and prevent the code from running.

```javascript
// Syntax error: Missing closing parenthesis

console.log("Hello, World";
```

- **Runtime Errors:** These occur while the code is executing and are often caused by unexpected conditions or invalid operations.

```
// Runtime error: Division by zero

const result = 10 / 0;
```

- **Logical Errors:** These are the hardest to detect because the code runs without errors, but it doesn't produce the expected output due to flawed logic.

```
// Logical error: Incorrect variable assignment

const total = 10 + 5;

console.log("Total: " + total); // Output: Total: 105
```

2. The try...catch Statement

The try...catch statement is used to handle exceptions (runtime errors) gracefully. It allows you to execute code within a try block and provide a fallback action in case an error occurs.

```
try {

// Code that might throw an error

const result = 10 / 0;

console.log(result);

} catch (error) {

// Handle the error

console.error("An error occurred: " + error.message);
```

```
}
```

In this example, the division by zero operation would normally throw an error, but the try...catch block prevents the program from crashing, and the error message is displayed.

3. The throw Statement

You can manually throw custom errors using the throw statement. This is useful when you want to handle specific cases or provide more meaningful error messages.

```
function divide(a, b) {

if (b === 0) {

throw new Error("Division by zero is not allowed.");

}

return a / b;

}

try {

const result = divide(10, 0);

console.log(result);

} catch (error) {

console.error("An error occurred: " + error.message);

}
```

Here, the divide function throws a custom error if the denominator is zero, leading to a more informative error message.

4. The finally Block

The try...catch statement can be extended with a finally block, which is executed regardless of whether an error occurred or not. This block is often used for cleanup tasks.

```javascript
try {

// Code that might throw an error

const result = 10 / 2;

console.log(result);

} catch (error) {

// Handle the error

console.error("An error occurred: " + error.message);

} finally {

// Cleanup code

console.log("Execution complete.");

}
```

In this example, the finally block ensures that the "Execution complete" message is always logged, regardless of whether an error occurred.

5. Debugging Tools

Debugging is the process of identifying and fixing errors in your code. JavaScript provides a range of debugging tools, including browser developer tools and integrated development environments (IDEs) like Visual Studio Code.

• **Console:** The console object provides methods like log, error, and info for printing messages and debugging information to the console.

console.log("Debugging message.");

• **Breakpoints:** You can set breakpoints in your code using your browser's developer tools or an IDE. Breakpoints pause code execution, allowing you to inspect variables and step through code line by line.

• **Watch and Variables Panel:** In developer tools, you can monitor the values of variables using the Watch panel. It's helpful for tracking the state of your code during execution.

• **Console Errors:** The console in developer tools displays error messages, making it easier to identify issues. Clicking on the error message often takes you to the line causing the error.

• **Step Through Code:** Debugging tools allow you to step through your code one line at a time, helping you trace the flow and find errors.

6. Using console.assert

The console.assert method is useful for adding assertions to your code. If an assertion is false, it throws an error with an optional error message.

const value = 5;

console.assert(value === 10, "Value should be 10.");

If value is not equal to 10, an error message is displayed in the console.

7. Debugging Tips

Here are some additional debugging tips:

- Use descriptive variable and function names to make it easier to understand your code.

- Break your code into smaller functions with single responsibilities. This makes it easier to isolate and debug issues.

- Comment your code to explain complex logic or why you made certain design decisions.

- Test your code incrementally and write unit tests to catch errors early.

- Take advantage of debugging features in your IDE, like auto-completion and code navigation.

Debugging is a skill that improves with practice. The more you debug, the more adept you become at identifying and fixing errors efficiently, resulting in more robust and reliable JavaScript code.

Chapter 6: JavaScript Libraries and Frameworks

6.1 Introduction to Popular JavaScript Libraries

JavaScript libraries and frameworks are essential tools for developers, offering pre-built solutions and abstractions to simplify common tasks and streamline development. In this section, we'll introduce you to some of the most popular JavaScript libraries and frameworks used in web development.

1. jQuery

jQuery[1] is a fast, small, and feature-rich JavaScript library. It simplifies HTML document traversal, event handling, animations, and AJAX interactions for rapid web development. jQuery provides a concise and powerful way to manipulate the DOM and handle events.

// Example: Using jQuery to handle a click event

```javascript
$(document).ready(function () {

$("button").click(function () {

alert("Button clicked!");

});

});
```

---

1. https://jquery.com/

2. React

React[2] is a widely-used JavaScript library for building user interfaces. Developed by Facebook, React allows you to create reusable UI components and efficiently update the DOM when data changes. It follows a component-based architecture.

// Example: Creating a simple React component

import React **from** 'react';

function MyComponent(props) {

return <div>Hello, {props.name}!</div>;

}

3. Angular

Angular[3] is a powerful and comprehensive framework for building web and mobile applications. Developed by Google, Angular provides features like two-way data binding, dependency injection, and a robust component-based architecture.

// Example: Creating an Angular component

import { Component } **from** '@angular/core';

@Component({

selector: 'app-root',

template: '<h1>Hello, {{ name }}</h1>',

})

---

2. https://reactjs.org/

3. https://angular.io/

```
export class AppComponent {

name = 'Angular';

}
```

4. Vue.js

Vue.js[4] is a progressive JavaScript framework for building user interfaces. It is known for its simplicity and flexibility. Vue allows you to incrementally adopt its features, making it suitable for both small projects and large-scale applications.

```
// Example: Creating a Vue component

<template>

<div>

<p>{{ message }}</p>

</div>

</template>

<script>

export default {

data() {

return {

message: 'Hello, Vue.js!',

};

},
```

---

4. https://vuejs.org/

```
};
```

```
</script>
```

5. Ember.js

Ember.js[5] is a robust and opinionated framework for building ambitious web applications. It follows the convention over configuration (CoC) and don't repeat yourself (DRY) principles, which promote consistency and productivity.

```
// Example: Creating an Ember.js component

import Component from '@glimmer/component';

export default class MyComponent extends Component {

message = 'Hello, Ember.js!';

}
```

6. Other Libraries and Frameworks

Apart from the ones mentioned above, there are many other JavaScript libraries and frameworks catering to specific needs, such as Backbone.js[6] for structuring web applications, Meteor[7] for full-stack development, D3.js[8] for data visualization, and Express.js[9] for building web servers.

Choosing the right library or framework depends on your project requirements, team expertise, and development goals. Each of these

5. https://emberjs.com/

6. https://backbonejs.org/

7. https://www.meteor.com/

8. https://d3js.org/

9. https://expressjs.com/

tools has its own strengths and use cases, so exploring and experimenting with them can enhance your web development skills.

6.2 Working with jQuery

jQuery[10] is a popular JavaScript library that simplifies DOM manipulation and event handling. It provides a convenient way to select elements, modify their attributes and content, and perform various actions on web pages. In this section, we will delve into how to work with jQuery effectively.

Getting Started with jQuery

To start using jQuery, you need to include it in your HTML file by adding the following script tag to your document's head or just before the closing body tag:

```
<script src="https://code.jquery.com/jquery-3.6.0.min.js"></script>
```

Once jQuery is included, you can use it to perform tasks like selecting elements, handling events, and modifying the DOM.

Selecting Elements

jQuery provides a powerful selection mechanism using CSS-style selectors. You can select elements by their tag name, class, ID, attributes, and more. For example:

```
// Select an element with an ID of 'my-element'

var element = $('#my-element');

// Select all elements with a class of 'btn'
```

---

10. https://jquery.com/

```
var buttons = $('.btn');
```

```
// Select all 'div' elements
```

```
var divs = $('div');
```

Modifying Elements

You can easily modify elements using jQuery. Common operations include changing text, attributes, and CSS styles. Here are some examples:

```
// Change the text of an element
```

```
$('#my-element').text('New text');
```

```
// Change an attribute (e.g., src of an image)
```

```
$('img').attr('src', 'new-image.jpg');
```

```
// Add a CSS class to an element
```

```
$('.btn').addClass('active');
```

Event Handling

jQuery simplifies event handling by allowing you to attach event listeners to elements easily. For instance:

```
// Attach a click event handler to a button element
```

```
$('#my-button').click(function () {
```

```
alert('Button clicked!');
```

```
});
```

```
// Shorthand for the click event
```

```javascript
$('#my-button').on('click', function () {

alert('Button clicked!');

});
```

Animations and Effects

jQuery includes various animation and effect functions to create smooth transitions and interactions on your webpage. You can animate properties like opacity, width, and height:

```javascript
// Animate the opacity of an element

$('#fade-me').animate({ opacity: 0.25 }, 1000);

// Toggle visibility with a sliding effect

$('#toggle-me').slideToggle(500);
```

AJAX with jQuery

jQuery simplifies making asynchronous requests (AJAX) to fetch data from a server or send data to it. You can use functions like $.ajax() or shortcuts like $.get() and $.post().

```javascript
// Using $.get() to fetch data from a server

$.get('https://api.example.com/data', function (data) {

console.log(data);

});

// Using $.post() to send data to a server

$.post('https://api.example.com/submit', { name: 'John', age: 30 },
function (response) {
```

```
console.log(response);
```

```
});
```

Plugins and Extensibility

One of the strengths of jQuery is its extensive ecosystem of plugins and extensions. These plugins provide additional functionality, such as sliders, carousels, and form validation. You can easily incorporate these plugins into your projects to save development time and add advanced features.

In summary, jQuery is a versatile and widely-used JavaScript library that simplifies web development tasks. Whether you're selecting elements, handling events, animating content, or making AJAX requests, jQuery provides a user-friendly API to enhance your web development experience.

6.3 React: Building User Interfaces

React[11] is a popular JavaScript library for building user interfaces. Developed and maintained by Facebook, React has gained widespread adoption in the web development community due to its component-based architecture and efficient way of managing the DOM.

Introduction to React

React focuses on the concept of components. Components are self-contained, reusable building blocks for creating user interfaces. They allow you to break down your UI into smaller, manageable pieces, making your code more maintainable and understandable.

Here's a simple example of a React component:

---

11. https://reactjs.org/

```javascript
import React from 'react';

class HelloWorld extends React.Component {

render() {

return <div>Hello, World!</div>;

}

}
```

In this example, HelloWorld is a React component that renders a simple "Hello, World!" message.

Virtual DOM

One of the key features of React is its Virtual DOM. React maintains a lightweight in-memory representation of the actual DOM. When data changes, React creates a new Virtual DOM tree, compares it with the previous one, and efficiently updates only the parts of the real DOM that have changed. This approach significantly improves performance and reduces the number of direct DOM manipulations.

JSX: JavaScript + XML

React uses JSX (JavaScript XML) syntax to define the structure of components. JSX allows you to write HTML-like code directly in your JavaScript files. Babel, a JavaScript compiler, transforms JSX code into regular JavaScript that browsers can understand.

Here's an example of JSX code within a React component:

```javascript
class Greeting extends React.Component {

render() {
```

```
return <h1>Hello, {this.props.name}!</h1>;

}

}
```

Component-Based Architecture

React encourages the decomposition of UI into reusable components. You can create complex UIs by composing these components together. Each component can have its state, properties (props), and lifecycle methods.

```
class Counter extends React.Component {

constructor(props) {

super(props);

this.state = { count: 0 };

}

increment = () => {

this.setState({ count: this.state.count + 1 });

};

render() {

return (

<div>

<p>Count: {this.state.count}</p>

<button onClick={this.increment}>Increment</button>
```

```
</div>

);

}

}
```

In this example, the Counter component manages its internal state and renders a count that can be incremented by clicking a button.

Unidirectional Data Flow

React follows a unidirectional data flow. Data flows from parent components to child components via props. Child components can communicate with parent components by triggering functions passed as props.

```
class Parent extends React.Component {

constructor(props) {

super(props);

this.state = { message: " };

}

handleMessageChange = (newMessage) => {

this.setState({ message: newMessage });

};

render() {

return (

<div>
```

```
<Child

message={this.state.message}

onMessageChange={this.handleMessageChange}

/>

</div>

);

}

}
```

In this example, the Parent component passes a message prop to the Child component and defines a callback function (onMessageChange) that the Child can call to update the message in the Parent.

React Ecosystem

React has a rich ecosystem with tools and libraries that complement its capabilities. For example, React Router[12] helps with routing in single-page applications, Redux[13] is commonly used for state management, and Material-UI[14] provides pre-designed UI components for a consistent look and feel.

React's versatility and active community make it a valuable choice for building user interfaces in modern web applications. Whether you're developing a single-page app or a complex web application,

---

12. https://reactrouter.com/

13. https://redux.js.org/

14. https://mui.com/

React's component-based approach and performance optimizations can help you create efficient and maintainable user interfaces.

6.4 Angular: Creating Dynamic Web Apps

Angular[15] is a comprehensive and powerful framework for building dynamic web applications. Developed by Google and maintained by a community of developers, Angular provides a structured approach to web development, making it suitable for creating complex and maintainable applications.

Introduction to Angular

Angular is built on the concept of components, similar to React. Each component is a self-contained building block of the application's user interface. Components encapsulate HTML templates, CSS styles, and TypeScript code, promoting modularity and reusability.

Here's a basic example of an Angular component:

```
import { Component } from '@angular/core';

@Component({

selector: 'app-hello-world',

template: '<h1>Hello, World!</h1>',

})

export class HelloWorldComponent {}
```

In this example, the HelloWorldComponent defines a simple template with an "Hello, World!" message.

---

15. https://angular.io/

TypeScript

Angular is primarily written in TypeScript, a statically-typed superset of JavaScript. TypeScript provides features like strong typing, interfaces, and decorators that enhance code quality and tooling support.

```
class Person {

constructor(public name: string, public age: number) {}

}

const person = new Person('John', 30);

console.log(person.name); // Outputs: John
```

TypeScript helps catch errors at compile time and improves code maintainability, making it a valuable choice for building large-scale applications.

Dependency Injection

Angular uses a robust dependency injection system to manage the instantiation and sharing of application components and services. This pattern promotes loose coupling, testability, and modularity.

```
import { Injectable } from '@angular/core';

@Injectable({

providedIn: 'root',

})
export class DataService {

getData() {
```

```
return 'Some data from DataService';

}

}
```

In this example, the DataService is marked as injectable and can be easily injected into other components or services.

Two-Way Data Binding

Angular supports two-way data binding, allowing data synchronization between the UI and application logic. Changes made in the UI reflect in the application state, and vice versa.

```
import { Component } from '@angular/core';

@Component({

selector: 'app-counter',

template: `

<input [(ngModel)]="count" />

<p>Count: {{ count }}</p>

`,

})

export class CounterComponent {

count = 0;

}
```

In this example, changes in the input field are automatically reflected in the count property, and changes to count are reflected in the UI.

Routing and Navigation

Angular provides a powerful routing system for building single-page applications (SPAs). You can define routes, route parameters, and navigate between different views within your application.

```typescript
import { RouterModule, Routes } from '@angular/router';

const routes: Routes = [

{ path: '', component: HomeComponent },

{ path: 'about', component: AboutComponent },

];

@NgModule({

imports: [RouterModule.forRoot(routes)],

exports: [RouterModule],

})

export class AppRoutingModule {}
```

In this example, the RouterModule is used to configure routes for a simple SPA with home and about pages.

Reactive Forms

Angular offers a reactive forms module for building complex forms with dynamic validation and state management.

```typescript
import { FormBuilder, FormGroup, Validators } from '@angular/forms';

export class LoginComponent {
```

```
loginForm: FormGroup;

constructor(private fb: FormBuilder) {

this.loginForm = fb.group({

username: ['', Validators.required],

password: ['', Validators.required],

});

}

onSubmit() {

// Handle form submission

}

}
```

In this example, the loginForm is defined with form controls and validators, making it easy to handle user input.

Angular CLI

The Angular CLI (Command Line Interface)[16] simplifies project setup, development, and deployment tasks. It provides commands for generating components, services, modules, and more.

```
# Create a new Angular project

ng new my-app

# Generate a new component

ng generate component my-component
```

---

16. https://cli.angular.io/

 # Start the development server

ng serve

The Angular CLI streamlines the development workflow and offers built-in testing, linting, and optimization tools.

Angular Ecosystem

Angular's ecosystem includes libraries and extensions like NgRx[17] for state management, Angular Material[18] for pre-designed UI components, and Angular Universal[19] for server-side rendering. These tools enhance Angular's capabilities and help developers build robust web applications.

In summary, Angular is a comprehensive framework for creating dynamic web applications with features like components, dependency injection, two-way data binding, routing, and forms. Its extensive ecosystem and TypeScript support make it a powerful choice for large-scale projects.

6.5 Vue.js: The Progressive JavaScript Framework

Vue.js[20] is a progressive JavaScript framework for building user interfaces. It is often praised for its simplicity, flexibility, and ease of integration into existing projects. Vue.js is suitable for both small, single-page applications and large, complex web applications.

---

17. https://ngrx.io/

18. https://material.angular.io/

19. https://angular.io/guide/universal

20. https://vuejs.org/

Introduction to Vue.js

Vue.js was created by Evan You and has gained rapid adoption within the web development community. It focuses on the view layer of an application and is designed to be incrementally adoptable. You can use Vue.js as a library to add interactive features to a single page or as a full-fledged framework for building complex applications.

Here's a basic example of a Vue.js component:

```
<template>

<div>

<p>{{ message }}</p>

<button @click="changeMessage">Change Message</button>

</div>

</template>

<script>

export default {

data() {

return {

message: 'Hello, Vue.js!',

};

},

methods: {

changeMessage() {
```

```
this.message = 'New Message';

},

},

};
```

```
</script>
```

In this example, a Vue.js component defines a template, data, and methods for handling user interactions.

Component-Based Architecture

Vue.js follows a component-based architecture similar to React and Angular. Components in Vue.js are reusable and encapsulate HTML templates, JavaScript logic, and CSS styles.

```
<template>

<div>

<h2>{{ title }}</h2>

<ul>

<li v-for="item in items" :key="item.id">{{ item.name }}</li>

</ul>

</div>

</template>

<script>

export default {
```

```
props: {

title: String,

items: Array,

},

};

</script>
```

In this example, a Vue.js component takes title and items as props and renders a list of items.

Vue Router

Vue Router is a powerful routing library that integrates seamlessly with Vue.js, enabling you to build single-page applications with multiple views. You can define routes, navigate between views, and pass route parameters.

```
import Vue from 'vue';

import VueRouter from 'vue-router';

import Home from './components/Home.vue';

import About from './components/About.vue';

Vue.use(VueRouter);

const routes = [

{ path: '/', component: Home },

{ path: '/about', component: About },

];
```

```
const router = new VueRouter({

routes,

});

new Vue({

router,

render: (h) => h(App),

}).$mount('#app');
```

In this example, Vue Router is used to configure routes for a Vue.js application with home and about pages.

Vue CLI

The Vue CLI[21] is a command-line tool that simplifies project setup, development, and deployment. It offers features like project generation, development server, and building for production.

```
# Create a new Vue.js project

vue create my-app

# Start the development server

vue serve

# Build for production

vue build
```

Vue CLI streamlines the development process and provides a consistent project structure.

---

21. https://cli.vuejs.org/

Vuex for State Management

For state management in Vue.js applications, Vuex[22] is a popular choice. It centralizes the storage of shared data and provides a predictable state management pattern.

```javascript
import Vue from 'vue';

import Vuex from 'vuex';

Vue.use(Vuex);

export default new Vuex.Store({

state: {

count: 0,

},

mutations: {

increment(state) {

state.count++;

},

},

actions: {

incrementAsync({ commit }) {

setTimeout(() => {

commit('increment');
```

---

22. https://vuex.vuejs.org/

```
}, 1000);

},

},

});
```

In this example, a Vuex store is created to manage the count state, and mutations and actions are defined to modify it.

Vue.js Ecosystem

Vue.js has a growing ecosystem with libraries and tools that enhance its capabilities. Libraries like Vue Router[23] for routing, Vuetify[24] for UI components, and Nuxt.js[25] for server-side rendering are commonly used with Vue.js to build robust web applications.

Vue.js is often praised for its gentle learning curve, which makes it accessible to both beginners and experienced developers. It is a versatile framework that can be used to build various types of applications, from simple interactive pages to large-scale, data-driven applications. Its simplicity, flexibility, and performance make it a valuable choice for web development projects.

---

23. https://router.vuejs.org/

24. https://vuetifyjs.com/

25. https://nuxtjs.org/

7.1 Node.js: An Introduction

Node.js[1] is a powerful and popular runtime environment that allows you to run JavaScript code on the server-side. It is built on the V8 JavaScript engine from Google and is designed for building scalable and high-performance network applications.

What is Node.js?

Node.js is not a programming language but a runtime environment that allows you to execute JavaScript code outside of the web browser. This means you can use JavaScript for server-side scripting, enabling you to create web servers, APIs, and a wide range of networked applications.

Node.js has a non-blocking, event-driven architecture that makes it well-suited for handling I/O-bound operations, such as reading and writing files, making network requests, and interacting with databases. This non-blocking nature allows Node.js to efficiently handle many concurrent connections without using a thread for each connection, which is common in traditional server-side technologies.

Features of Node.js

1. **Single Threaded and Event-Driven**: Node.js uses a single-threaded event loop for handling asynchronous operations, making it highly efficient in handling many concurrent connections.

2. **V8 JavaScript Engine**: Node.js is built on the V8 JavaScript engine, which is known for its high performance and optimization capabilities.

---

1. https://nodejs.org/

3. **NPM (Node Package Manager)**: Node.js comes with npm, a package manager that allows you to easily install and manage third-party libraries and modules.
4. **CommonJS Modules**: Node.js uses the CommonJS module system, which allows you to organize your code into reusable modules and manage dependencies.
5. **Cross-Platform**: Node.js is available for various operating systems, including Windows, macOS, and Linux, making it a cross-platform solution.
6. **Large Ecosystem**: Node.js has a vast ecosystem of open-source libraries and frameworks that simplify building web applications, APIs, and more.

Hello World in Node.js

Let's create a simple "Hello, World!" application in Node.js to get started:

```javascript
// Import the 'http' module for creating an HTTP server

const http = require('http');

// Create an HTTP server that responds with 'Hello, World!' for all requests

const server = http.createServer((req, res) => {

res.writeHead(200, { 'Content-Type': 'text/plain' });

res.end('Hello, World!\n');

});

// Listen on port 3000

server.listen(3000, 'localhost', () => {
```

```javascript
console.log('Server is running at http://localhost:3000/');
```

```javascript
});
```

In this example, we import the http module, create an HTTP server, and listen on port 3000. When you run this script, it will start a server that responds with "Hello, World!" when you access it in a web browser.

Building APIs with Node.js

Node.js is often used for building APIs (Application Programming Interfaces) that serve data to web and mobile applications. You can use frameworks like Express.js to simplify API development. Here's a basic example of creating an API endpoint using Express.js:

```javascript
const express = require('express');
```

```javascript
const app = express();
```

```javascript
const port = 3000;
```

```javascript
// Define a route that responds with a JSON message
```

```javascript
app.get('/api/hello', (req, res) => {
```

```javascript
res.json({ message: 'Hello, API!' });
```

```javascript
});
```

```javascript
// Start the server
```

```javascript
app.listen(port, () => {
```

```javascript
console.log(`API server is running on port ${port}`);
```

```javascript
});
```

In this example, we use Express.js to create a simple API with a single route that responds with a JSON message when accessed.

Node.js is a versatile and widely adopted technology for server-side development. Whether you are building web servers, APIs, or real-time applications, Node.js provides the tools and performance you need to create robust and scalable solutions. It has a thriving ecosystem and a vibrant community, making it a valuable skill for developers.

7.2 Creating a Simple Node.js Server

In this section, we'll explore how to create a basic Node.js server. Node.js makes it easy to build web servers to handle HTTP requests and responses. You can create a server using the built-in http module, which provides the necessary functionality for handling HTTP communication.

Setting Up a Node.js Server

To create a Node.js server, follow these steps:

1. Import the http module:

```
const http = require('http');
```

1. Create an HTTP server by calling http.createServer() and passing a callback function that will be executed whenever a request is received. This callback function takes two parameters, req (the request object) and res (the response object):

```
const server = http.createServer((req, res) => {
```

```
// Your code for handling requests and generating responses goes here

});
```

1. Inside the callback function, you can define how the server should respond to different types of requests. For example, you can set the response headers and send a response body:

```
res.writeHead(200, { 'Content-Type': 'text/plain' });

res.end('Hello, Node.js Server!');
```

1. Specify the port and hostname where your server should listen for incoming requests. You can use server.listen() for this purpose:

```
const port = 3000;

const hostname = 'localhost';

server.listen(port, hostname, () => {

console.log(`Server running at http://${hostname}:${port}/`);

});
```

Example: Creating a Simple HTTP Server

Here's a complete example of creating a simple HTTP server that listens on port 3000 and responds with "Hello, Node.js Server!" to all incoming requests:

```
const http = require('http');

const server = http.createServer((req, res) => {

res.writeHead(200, { 'Content-Type': 'text/plain' });
```

```
res.end('Hello, Node.js Server!');

});

const port = 3000;

const hostname = 'localhost';

server.listen(port, hostname, () => {

console.log(`Server running at http://${hostname}:${port}/`);

});
```

You can run this script using Node.js, and your server will be accessible at http://localhost:3000/. When you access this URL in a web browser or make a GET request using a tool like curl, you'll receive the "Hello, Node.js Server!" response.

This is a basic example of creating an HTTP server in Node.js. In practice, you can use various libraries and frameworks like Express.js to build more complex and feature-rich web servers for your applications.

7.3 NPM: Node Package Manager

NPM[2], short for Node Package Manager, is a widely-used package manager for JavaScript development. It comes bundled with Node.js, making it the default package manager for Node.js applications. NPM simplifies the process of installing, managing, and sharing packages (libraries and modules) for your Node.js projects.

Installing NPM

If you have Node.js installed, NPM should already be available on your system. You can check the version of NPM by running the following command in your terminal:

```
npm -v
```

To update NPM to the latest version, you can use the following command:

```
npm install -g npm
```

Package.json

In Node.js projects, you typically start by creating a package.json file in the root directory of your project. This file serves as a manifest for your project and includes important information such as project name, version, dependencies, and scripts.

You can create a package.json file interactively by running:

```
npm init
```

Follow the prompts to provide the necessary information about your project, or you can create a package.json file with default values by adding the -y flag:

```
npm init -y
```

Here's an example of a simple package.json file:

```
{
"name": "my-node-app",
"version": "1.0.0",
```

"description": "A simple Node.js application",

"main": "index.js",

"scripts": {

"start": "node index.js"

},

"dependencies": {

"express": "^4.17.1"

}

}

In this example, we have specified the project name, version, description, entry point (main), scripts, and dependencies. The dependencies section lists the packages required for the project, along with their versions.

Installing Dependencies

To install the dependencies listed in your package.json file, you can use the npm install command. For example, to install the express package mentioned in the previous package.json example, you would run:

npm install

This command will install all the dependencies specified in your package.json file into a node_modules directory in your project.

Managing Dependencies

You can add new dependencies to your project by running npm install package-name. For example:

npm install lodash

To save a dependency as a project dependency, you can use the —save flag (or its shorthand -S):

npm install lodash—save

To save a dependency as a development dependency (used during development and testing), you can use the —save-dev flag (or its shorthand -D):

npm install mocha—save-dev

Running Scripts

In your package.json, you can define scripts that can be executed using the npm run command. For example, the following package.json includes a "start" script that runs the node index.js command:

```
{

"scripts": {

"start": "node index.js"

}

}
```

You can run this script using:

npm run start

NPM is a vital tool in the Node.js ecosystem. It simplifies dependency management, allows you to share your projects with others, and provides an efficient way to define and run project-specific scripts. Understanding how to use NPM effectively is essential for Node.js developers.

7.4 Building RESTful APIs with Express

Express.js[3] is a popular and minimalistic web application framework for Node.js. It simplifies the process of building web applications and RESTful APIs by providing a robust set of features and a straightforward, flexible API. In this section, we'll explore how to build RESTful APIs using Express.

Installing Express

Before you can start using Express, you need to install it as a dependency in your Node.js project. You can do this using NPM, as follows:

npm install express

Creating an Express Application

To create an Express application, you typically start by requiring the Express module and creating an instance of it. Here's a minimal example:

const express = require('express');

const app = express();

const port = 3000;

---

3. https://expressjs.com/

In this example, we've imported the Express module, created an instance of the Express application, and specified the port on which the server will listen.

Defining Routes

In Express, routes are used to define how your application responds to HTTP requests. You can define routes for various HTTP methods (GET, POST, PUT, DELETE, etc.) and URL patterns. Here's an example of defining a simple GET route that responds with "Hello, Express!" when the root URL is accessed:

```
app.get('/', (req, res) => {

res.send('Hello, Express!');

});
```

Starting the Server

To start your Express application and make it listen for incoming requests, you use the app.listen() method:

```
app.listen(port, () => {

console.log(`Server is listening at http://localhost:${port}`);

});
```

Running the Express Application

After defining your routes and starting the server, you can run your Express application using Node.js. Save the code in a file (e.g., app.js) and run the following command:

```
node app.js
```

Your Express application will now be accessible at http://localhost:3000/, and it will respond with "Hello, Express!" when you access the root URL.

Handling Different HTTP Methods

Express allows you to handle different HTTP methods using corresponding functions. For example, to handle a POST request, you can use app.post(), and to handle a PUT request, you can use app.put(). Here's an example of handling a POST request:

```
app.post('/api/data', (req, res) => {

// Process the POST data and send a response

res.json({ message: 'Data received!' });

});
```

Middleware in Express

Middleware functions are an essential part of Express. They are functions that have access to the request (req) and response (res) objects and can modify them. Middleware functions can be used to perform tasks such as logging, authentication, parsing request bodies, and more.

```
// Middleware function to log incoming requests

app.use((req, res, next) => {

console.log(`Request received at ${new Date()}`);

next(); // Call the next middleware function

});
```

Error Handling

Express provides mechanisms for handling errors. You can define error-handling middleware functions that are executed when an error occurs. This allows you to centralize error handling and provide meaningful responses to clients.

```
// Error-handling middleware function

app.use((err, req, res, next) => {

console.error(err.stack);

res.status(500).send('Something broke!');

});
```

Express is a powerful framework for building web applications and RESTful APIs in Node.js. Its simplicity, flexibility, and extensive ecosystem of middleware make it a popular choice among developers. By following the principles of REST and using Express, you can create scalable and robust APIs for your web and mobile applications.

7.5 Real-Time Applications with WebSocket

WebSocket is a communication protocol that provides full-duplex, bidirectional communication channels over a single TCP connection. Unlike traditional HTTP requests, WebSocket allows real-time, low-latency communication between clients and servers. In this section, we'll explore how to implement real-time applications with WebSocket using the popular library Socket.io[4] and Node.js.

---

4. https://socket.io/

Installing Socket.io

To use Socket.io in your Node.js project, you first need to install it as a dependency using NPM:

npm install socket.io

Setting Up a WebSocket Server

In Node.js, you can set up a WebSocket server alongside your HTTP server using Socket.io. Here's an example of setting up a basic WebSocket server:

const http = require('http');

const express = require('express');

const app = express();

const server = http.createServer(app);

const io = require('socket.io')(server);

const port = 3000;

// Serve a basic HTML page

app.get('/', (req, res) => {

res.sendFile(__dirname + '/index.html');

});

// Handle WebSocket connections

io.on('connection', (socket) => {

console.log('A user connected');

```javascript
// Handle messages from clients
socket.on('chat message', (message) => {

console.log('Message from client: ' + message);

io.emit('chat message', message); // Broadcast the message to all connected clients

});

// Handle disconnections
socket.on('disconnect', () => {

console.log('A user disconnected');

});

});

server.listen(port, () => {

console.log(`Server is listening on http://localhost:${port}`);

});
```

Creating a WebSocket Client

To communicate with the WebSocket server from the client side, you can use Socket.io's JavaScript library. Include the library in your HTML file as follows:

```html
<script src="/socket.io/socket.io.js"></script>
```

Then, create a WebSocket connection on the client side and send messages to the server:

```javascript
const socket = io();
```

```
// Send a message to the server

socket.emit('chat message', 'Hello, WebSocket Server!');

// Receive messages from the server

socket.on('chat message', (message) => {

console.log('Message from server: ' + message);

});
```

Broadcasting Messages

One of the advantages of WebSocket is the ability to broadcast messages to all connected clients in real-time. In the server code example above, when a message is received from a client (socket.on('chat message', ...)), the server uses io.emit() to broadcast that message to all connected clients.

Broadcasting to Specific Clients

Socket.io allows you to send messages to specific clients or groups of clients by using room functionality and specifying custom namespaces. This is useful for implementing private messaging or grouping clients with similar interests.

Real-Time Applications

WebSocket is a fundamental technology for building real-time applications such as chat applications, online gaming, collaborative editing tools, and more. The ability to push updates and notifications to clients in real-time greatly enhances the user experience and opens up new possibilities for interactive web applications.

Socket.io simplifies the implementation of WebSocket-based communication in Node.js applications, making it accessible to developers who want to add real-time features to their projects. Whether you're building a simple chat application or a complex multiplayer game, WebSocket and Socket.io can be powerful tools in your toolkit.

8.1 Working with JSON Data

JavaScript Object Notation (JSON) is a lightweight data interchange format that is easy for humans to read and write, and easy for machines to parse and generate. It has become the standard for data exchange on the web and is widely used for configuration files, data storage, and API responses. In this section, we'll explore how to work with JSON data in JavaScript.

JSON Basics

JSON data is represented as a collection of key-value pairs, similar to JavaScript objects. Here's an example of a simple JSON object:

```
{

"name": "John Doe",

"age": 30,

"email": "john@example.com"

}
```

In JavaScript, you can parse a JSON string into an object using the JSON.parse() method:

```
const jsonString = '{"name": "John Doe", "age": 30, "email": "john@example.com"}';
```

```javascript
const jsonObject = JSON.parse(jsonString);

console.log(jsonObject.name); // Output: John Doe

console.log(jsonObject.age); // Output: 30
```

Conversely, you can stringify a JavaScript object into a JSON string using the JSON.stringify() method:

```javascript
const person = {

name: "Jane Smith",

age: 25,

email: "jane@example.com"

};

const jsonString = JSON.stringify(person);

console.log(jsonString); // Output: {"name":"Jane Smith","age":25,"email":"jane@example.com"}
```

Parsing JSON Data

When working with data retrieved from external sources, such as API responses, you often receive JSON data as a string. To work with this data in JavaScript, you should parse it into an object using JSON.parse(). Here's an example of parsing JSON data from an API response:

```javascript
const fetch = require('node-fetch'); // Import the 'node-fetch' library for making HTTP requests

fetch('https://api.example.com/data')

.then((response) => response.json())
```

```javascript
.then((data) => {

console.log(data); // Parsed JSON data

})

.catch((error) => {

console.error('Error:', error);

});
```

Creating JSON Data

When you need to create JSON data in JavaScript, you can start with a JavaScript object and use JSON.stringify() to convert it into a JSON string. For instance, you can create complex data structures and then serialize them into JSON for storage or transmission:

```javascript
const book = {

title: "The Great Gatsby",

author: "F. Scott Fitzgerald",

publicationYear: 1925,

genres: ["Classics", "Fiction"],

isAvailable: true

};

const jsonBook = JSON.stringify(book);

console.log(jsonBook);
```

JSON Schema and Validation

JSON Schema is a vocabulary for defining the structure of JSON data. It allows you to specify constraints on what data is valid and what data is not. Various libraries and tools are available for validating JSON data against a schema, ensuring data integrity and compliance with specific data formats.

Using JSON in Web APIs

JSON is a common format for data exchange in web APIs. When designing or consuming APIs, it's essential to understand how data is represented in JSON format and how to work with it in your JavaScript code. Many JavaScript frameworks and libraries provide convenient methods for making API requests and handling JSON responses.

Working with JSON data is a fundamental skill for web developers, as it enables you to exchange and manipulate data effectively in various applications, from web development to server-side programming and data analysis. Whether you're parsing JSON data from APIs or creating JSON objects to store and transmit information, JSON is a versatile and widely used data format in the world of web development.

8.2 AJAX and Fetch API

Asynchronous JavaScript and XML (AJAX) is a set of web development techniques that allow you to make asynchronous HTTP requests from a web page to a server without having to reload the entire page. It enables you to fetch data, send data, and update parts of a web page dynamically, providing a smoother and more interactive user experience. In this section, we'll explore AJAX and the modern Fetch API for making asynchronous HTTP requests in JavaScript.

The Basics of AJAX

AJAX is not a programming language or a specific technology but rather a concept that uses a combination of several technologies, including:

- JavaScript: To create and manage asynchronous requests.

- XMLHttpRequest: An object that allows you to send HTTP requests and receive responses.

- DOM (Document Object Model): To manipulate the web page and update its content.

Here's a simple example of an AJAX request using the XMLHttpRequest object:

```javascript
const xhr = new XMLHttpRequest();

xhr.open('GET', 'https://api.example.com/data', true); // Specify the request method, URL, and asynchronous flag

xhr.onreadystatechange = function () {

if (xhr.readyState === 4 && xhr.status === 200) {

const response = JSON.parse(xhr.responseText); // Parse the JSON response

console.log(response);

}
```

```
};
```

xhr.send(); // *Send the request*

The Fetch API

The Fetch API is a modern and more flexible way to make HTTP requests in JavaScript. It provides a promise-based interface that simplifies the process of sending and handling HTTP requests. Here's an example of a GET request using the Fetch API:

```
fetch('https://api.example.com/data')

.then((response) => {

if (!response.ok) {

throw new Error('Network response was not ok');

}

return response.json(); // Parse the JSON response

})

.then((data) => {

console.log(data);

})

.catch((error) => {

console.error('Error:', error);

});
```

The Fetch API supports various request methods, including GET, POST, PUT, DELETE, and more. You can also specify request headers, pass data in the request body, and handle various response types, such as JSON, text, and binary data.

Making POST Requests

To send data to a server, you can use the Fetch API to make POST requests. Here's an example of sending JSON data in a POST request:

```
const postData = {

name: 'John Doe',

email: 'john@example.com',

};

fetch('https://api.example.com/postData', {

method: 'POST',

headers: {

'Content-Type': 'application/json',

},

body: JSON.stringify(postData), // Convert JavaScript object to
JSON string

})

.then((response) => {

if (!response.ok) {

throw new Error('Network response was not ok');

}
```

```
return response.json();

})

.then((data) => {

console.log(data);

})

.catch((error) => {

console.error('Error:', error);

});
```

Cross-Origin Requests

When making AJAX requests to a different domain than the one serving your web page (cross-origin requests), you might encounter cross-origin resource sharing (CORS) restrictions. CORS is a security feature implemented by browsers to prevent unauthorized access to resources on different domains. To make cross-origin requests, the server you are requesting data from must support CORS and include the appropriate response headers.

Fetch API vs. XMLHttpRequest

The Fetch API has become the preferred choice for making HTTP requests due to its modern, promise-based syntax and improved functionality. However, XMLHttpRequest is still supported in older browsers and can be used when necessary.

In summary, AJAX and the Fetch API are essential tools for making asynchronous HTTP requests in JavaScript. Whether you need to fetch data from an API, send data to a server, or update parts of a web page without full page reloads, these techniques provide the foundation for creating dynamic and interactive web applications.

8.3 Consuming RESTful APIs

Representational State Transfer (REST) is an architectural style for designing networked applications. It relies on a stateless, client-server communication model and typically uses HTTP as the communication protocol. RESTful APIs (Application Programming Interfaces) are web services that adhere to REST principles and provide a way for clients to interact with server resources. In this section, we'll explore how to consume RESTful APIs using JavaScript.

Making GET Requests

Consuming a RESTful API often involves making HTTP GET requests to retrieve data from the server. JavaScript provides various methods and libraries for making these requests. One common approach is to use the Fetch API, which we discussed in the previous section. Here's an example of making a GET request to retrieve data from a RESTful API:

```javascript
fetch('https://api.example.com/posts')

.then((response) => {

if (!response.ok) {

throw new Error('Network response was not ok');

}

return response.json(); // Parse the JSON response

})
```

```
.then((data) => {

console.log(data); // Process the retrieved data

})

.catch((error) => {

console.error('Error:', error);

});
```

Handling Authentication

Many RESTful APIs require authentication to access protected resources. You can include authentication credentials, such as API keys or tokens, in your HTTP requests to authenticate with the API server. Here's an example of including an API key in a Fetch request:

```
const apiKey = 'your-api-key';

fetch('https://api.example.com/protected-resource', {

headers: {

Authorization: `Bearer ${apiKey}`,

},

})

.then((response) => {

if (!response.ok) {

throw new Error('Network response was not ok');

}
```

```javascript
return response.json();

})

.then((data) => {

console.log(data);

})

.catch((error) => {

console.error('Error:', error);

});
```

Making POST Requests

In addition to retrieving data, you may need to send data to a RESTful API by making HTTP POST requests. This is common when creating, updating, or deleting resources on the server. Here's an example of making a POST request to create a new resource:

```javascript
const newPost = {

title: 'New Post',

content: 'This is the content of the new post.',

};

fetch('https://api.exemple.com/posts', {

method: 'POST',

headers: {

'Content-Type': 'application/json',
```

```
    Authorization: `Bearer ${apiKey}`, // Include authentication
  },
  body: JSON.stringify(newPost),
})
  .then((response) => {
    if (!response.ok) {
      throw new Error('Network response was not ok');
    }
    return response.json();
  })
  .then((data) => {
    console.log(data);
  })
  .catch((error) => {
    console.error('Error:', error);
  });
```

Handling Errors

When consuming RESTful APIs, it's crucial to handle errors gracefully. HTTP responses can include status codes indicating success or failure, and you should check these status codes to handle errors properly. Additionally, many APIs provide detailed error messages or error codes in their response payloads, which you can use to provide informative error messages to users.

Rate Limiting and Pagination

Some RESTful APIs impose rate limits on the number of requests you can make in a given time period. It's essential to be aware of these limits and implement appropriate strategies, such as request throttling or pagination, to work within these limits when consuming the API.

Documentation and API Clients

API documentation is a valuable resource when consuming RESTful APIs. It provides information about available endpoints, request and response formats, authentication methods, and usage examples. Some APIs also offer client libraries or SDKs (Software Development Kits) for popular programming languages, making it easier to interact with the API.

In summary, consuming RESTful APIs is a fundamental skill for web developers, as it enables you to access and manipulate data from external sources, such as third-party services or your own server-side applications. Whether you're building a web application that integrates with external APIs or creating serverless functions that interact with RESTful services, understanding how to make HTTP requests and handle API responses is essential for modern web development.

8.4 Data Manipulation and Transformation

In web development, data manipulation and transformation are essential tasks when working with data retrieved from various sources, including APIs, databases, or user input. JavaScript provides a rich set of functions and methods for processing and transforming data efficiently. In this section, we'll explore common techniques and tools for data manipulation and transformation in JavaScript.

Arrays and Iteration

Arrays are a fundamental data structure in JavaScript, and they offer various methods for manipulating and transforming data. You can use methods like map(), filter(), reduce(), and forEach() to perform operations on arrays.

Example 1: Using map() to Transform Array Elements

```
const numbers = [1, 2, 3, 4, 5];

const doubledNumbers = numbers.map((number) => number * 2);

console.log(doubledNumbers); // [2, 4, 6, 8, 10]
```

Example 2: Using filter() to Filter Array Elements

```
const fruits = ['apple', 'banana', 'cherry', 'date', 'elderberry'];

const filteredFruits = fruits.filter((fruit) => fruit.length > 5);

console.log(filteredFruits); // ['banana', 'cherry', 'elderberry']
```

Example 3: Using reduce() to Aggregate Array Elements

```
const values = [1, 2, 3, 4, 5];

const sum = values.reduce((accumulator, currentValue) => accumulator + currentValue, 0);

console.log(sum); // 15
```

Object Transformation

When working with objects, you might need to transform their structure or extract specific properties. The map() function can also be used with objects to achieve this.

Example: Transforming an Array of Objects

```javascript
const products = [

{ id: 1, name: 'Product A', price: 10 },

{ id: 2, name: 'Product B', price: 20 },

{ id: 3, name: 'Product C', price: 30 },

];

const transformedProducts = products.map((product) => ({

productId: product.id,

productName: product.name,

}));

console.log(transformedProducts);
```

String Manipulation

JavaScript provides a wide range of string manipulation methods for tasks such as searching, replacing, splitting, and joining strings.

Example: Splitting and Joining Strings

```javascript
const sentence = 'This is a sample sentence';
```

```javascript
const words = sentence.split(' '); // Split the sentence into words

console.log(words); // ['This', 'is', 'a', 'sample', 'sentence']

const joinedSentence = words.join('-'); // Join words with hyphens

console.log(joinedSentence); // 'This-is-a-sample-sentence'
```

Data Validation and Sanitization

When working with user input or external data, data validation and sanitization are critical to ensure data integrity and security. You can use regular expressions and built-in functions to validate and sanitize data.

Example: Validating Email Addresses

```javascript
function isValidEmail(email) {

// Regular expression for email validation

const emailRegex = /^[A-Za-z0-9._%-]+@[A-Za-z0-9.-]+\.[A-Za-z]{2,4}$/;

return emailRegex.test(email);

}

console.log(isValidEmail('user@example.com')); // true

console.log(isValidEmail('invalid-email')); // false
```

JSON Manipulation

JavaScript Object Notation (JSON) is a common data format for exchanging data between a server and a client. You can parse JSON data into JavaScript objects and stringify JavaScript objects into JSON.

Example: Parsing and Stringifying JSON

const jsonData = '{"name": "John", "age": 30}';

const parsedData = JSON.parse(jsonData);

console.log(parsedData.name); // *'John'*

const jsObject = { name: 'Alice', age: 25 };

const jsonString = JSON.stringify(jsObject);

console.log(jsonString); // *'{"name":"Alice","age":25}'*

Data Transformation Libraries

In addition to built-in JavaScript methods, there are several libraries and frameworks that can simplify complex data manipulation and transformation tasks. Libraries like Lodash provide a wide range of utility functions for working with data collections, and tools like Moment.js help with date and time manipulation.

In summary, data manipulation and transformation are fundamental operations in web development, and JavaScript provides powerful tools and methods to handle these tasks efficiently. Whether you're processing arrays, transforming objects, manipulating strings, validating data, or working with JSON, a solid understanding of JavaScript's data manipulation capabilities is essential for building robust web applications.

8.5 Data Visualization with D3.js

Data visualization is a powerful way to convey complex information in a clear and intuitive manner. D3.js, short for Data-Driven Documents, is a JavaScript library that facilitates the creation of interactive and dynamic data visualizations on the web. It provides a flexible and expressive framework for binding data to the Document Object Model (DOM) and applying data-driven transformations to the document.

Introduction to D3.js

D3.js was created by Mike Bostock and has become a widely adopted library for data visualization. It enables developers to create a wide range of visualizations, including bar charts, line charts, scatter plots, heatmaps, and more. D3.js is built around the concept of data binding, where data elements are bound to DOM elements, and changes in the data are reflected in the document.

To get started with D3.js, you can include it in your HTML document using a script tag:

```
<script src="https://d3js.org/d3.v6.min.js"></script>
```

Basic Data Binding

One of the fundamental concepts in D3.js is data binding. You can use the data() method to bind data to a selection of DOM elements and the enter(), exit(), and update() methods to manage data changes.

Example: Binding Data to DOM Elements

```
const data = [10, 20, 30, 40, 50];
```

```
// Select all `div` elements in the document

const divs = d3.selectAll('div');

// Bind the data to the selection

const divWithData = divs.data(data);

// Enter: create new elements for data points that don't have
corresponding DOM elements

divWithData.enter().append('div');

// Update: update existing elements with new data

divWithData.text((d) => d);

// Exit: remove elements for data points that no longer exist

divWithData.exit().remove();
```

Creating SVG-Based Visualizations

Scalable Vector Graphics (SVG) is a popular format for creating graphics and visualizations in D3.js. You can use D3.js to create and manipulate SVG elements, such as rectangles, circles, and paths, to build various types of charts.

Example: Creating a Simple Bar Chart

```
const dataset = [5, 10, 15, 20, 25];

const svgWidth = 400;

const svgHeight = 200;

const barPadding = 5;
```

```javascript
const svg = d3.select('svg')

.attr('width', svgWidth)

.attr('height', svgHeight);

const barWidth = svgWidth / dataset.length;

const bars = svg.selectAll('rect')

.data(dataset)

.enter()

.append('rect')

.attr('x', (d, i) => i * barWidth)

.attr('y', (d) => svgHeight - d * 4)

.attr('width', barWidth - barPadding)

.attr('height', (d) => d * 4)

.attr('fill', 'blue');
```

Interactivity and Transitions

D3.js excels in creating interactive data visualizations. You can add interactivity by handling user events and creating smooth transitions when data changes.

Example: Adding a Click Event and Transition to Bar Chart

```javascript
bars.on('click', function (d) {

d3.select(this)
```

.transition()

.duration(1000)

.attr('fill', 'red');

});

D3.js Ecosystem

D3.js has a vibrant ecosystem with many plugins and extensions that simplify common visualization tasks. Some popular libraries built on top of D3.js include C3.js for chart generation, NVD3 for reusable charts, and dc.js for creating dashboards.

In summary, D3.js is a powerful library for creating data visualizations in web applications. Its data-driven approach, support for SVG, and rich set of features make it a valuable tool for conveying information effectively. Whether you need to build simple charts or complex interactive visualizations, D3.js provides the flexibility and capabilities to meet your needs.

9.1 Common Security Threats in Web Applications

Security is a critical aspect of web application development. Understanding common security threats is essential for building secure and reliable web applications. In this section, we'll explore some of the most prevalent security threats that web developers need to be aware of and how to mitigate them.

Cross-Site Scripting (XSS)

Cross-Site Scripting, often abbreviated as XSS, is a widespread security vulnerability that occurs when an attacker injects malicious scripts into web pages viewed by other users. These scripts can execute arbitrary code in the context of the victim's browser, leading to data theft, session hijacking, and more.

Mitigation Strategies for XSS

1. **Input Validation**: Ensure that all user inputs are properly validated and sanitized before rendering them on a web page. Use libraries and frameworks that automatically escape user-generated content.
2. **Content Security Policy (CSP)**: Implement CSP headers in your web application to specify which sources of content are allowed to be loaded. This can help prevent the execution of unauthorized scripts.
3. **Use Secure Cookies**: Set the HttpOnly and Secure flags on cookies to protect them from being accessed by JavaScript and to ensure they are only transmitted over secure (HTTPS) connections.
4. **Encode Output**: Encode user-generated content appropriately before rendering it on web pages. For example, use HTML entity encoding to prevent script execution.

Cross-Site Request Forgery (CSRF)

Cross-Site Request Forgery (CSRF) is an attack that tricks users into making unwanted and unauthorized actions on a different website while they are authenticated on another site. This can lead to actions like changing passwords, transferring funds, or updating settings without the user's consent.

Mitigation Strategies for CSRF

1. **Use Anti-CSRF Tokens**: Include anti-CSRF tokens in forms and verify them on the server side before processing requests. These tokens should be unique per user session.
2. **Same-Site Cookies**: Set the SameSite attribute on cookies to restrict their scope to the same site, preventing them from being sent in cross-site requests.
3. **Double-Submit Cookies**: Generate and compare a random cookie value with a request parameter. If they don't match, reject the request.

Content Security Policy (CSP)

Content Security Policy (CSP) is a security feature that helps prevent cross-site scripting (XSS) and other code injection attacks. It allows you to define a whitelist of trusted sources for content, scripts, and other resources.

Mitigation Strategies for CSP

1. **Implement a Strict CSP**: Configure a strict CSP that only allows content to be loaded from trusted sources. Avoid using unsafe inline scripts and styles.
2. **Report Violations**: Set up CSP reporting to receive reports of policy violations. This helps you identify and fix issues in your CSP.
3. **Test and Monitor**: Regularly test your CSP and monitor for any policy violations. Adjust the policy as needed to strike a balance between security and functionality.

SQL Injection

SQL Injection is a type of attack where an attacker inserts malicious SQL queries into an application's input fields, leading to unauthorized access to databases, data theft, and even data deletion.

Mitigation Strategies for SQL Injection

1. **Use Parameterized Statements**: Instead of building SQL queries by concatenating user inputs, use parameterized statements provided by your database library. These statements automatically sanitize inputs.
2. **Input Validation**: Validate and sanitize user inputs to ensure they do not contain malicious SQL code.
3. **Least Privilege Principle**: Limit database user permissions to only what is necessary for the application. Avoid using overly privileged database accounts.
4. **Error Handling**: Implement proper error handling and avoid exposing SQL errors to users. Log any unexpected errors for debugging.

These are just a few of the common security threats in web applications and some strategies to mitigate them. It's crucial to stay informed about emerging threats and security best practices to protect your web applications and user data. Security should be an ongoing concern throughout the development and maintenance lifecycle of your application.

9.2 Cross-Site Scripting (XSS) Prevention

Cross-Site Scripting (XSS) is a serious security vulnerability that allows attackers to inject malicious scripts into web pages viewed by other users. To prevent XSS attacks, web developers must implement various security measures.

Input Validation and Sanitization

One of the fundamental XSS prevention techniques is input validation and sanitization. Whenever your web application receives user inputs, ensure that you validate and sanitize them to remove any potentially harmful content. Libraries and frameworks often provide functions to perform these tasks.

Here's an example in JavaScript using a popular library called DOMPurify to sanitize user inputs:

```javascript
const DOMPurify = require('dompurify');

// Sanitize user input

const userInput = '<script>alert("XSS attack");</script>';

const sanitizedInput = DOMPurify.sanitize(userInput);

// Use sanitizedInput in your application
```

Content Security Policy (CSP)

Content Security Policy (CSP) is a security feature that helps prevent XSS attacks by defining a whitelist of trusted sources for content, scripts, and other resources. Implementing CSP headers in your web application's response can significantly enhance security.

Here's an example of setting up a basic CSP header in an HTTP response:

```javascript
// Set up Content Security Policy (CSP) header

app.use((req, res, next) => {
```

```
res.setHeader('Content-Security-Policy', "default-src 'self'");
```

```
next();
```

```
});
```

In this example, the default-src 'self' policy allows only resources from the same origin ('self') to be loaded. You can customize this policy to specify trusted sources for scripts, styles, images, and more.

Escape User-Generated Content

When rendering user-generated content, it's crucial to escape it properly to prevent any script execution. Most web frameworks and templating engines provide automatic escaping of content. For example, in a JavaScript-based template:

```
// Example using EJS template engine
```

```
const ejs = require('ejs');
```

```
const userContent = '<script>alert("XSS attack");</script>';
```

```
const template = `<div>${userContent}</div>`;
```

```
const renderedHTML = ejs.render(template);
```

```
// The userContent is escaped and will not execute as a script
```

HTTP-Only and Secure Cookies

Cookies that are marked as HTTP-Only cannot be accessed by JavaScript. This prevents attackers from stealing session cookies and executing XSS attacks. Additionally, secure cookies should only be transmitted over HTTPS connections.

```
// Set an HTTP-Only and Secure cookie in Express.js
```

```
res.cookie('session', '123456', { httpOnly: true, secure: true });
```

Use Trusted Libraries and Frameworks

When building web applications, it's essential to use trusted and well-maintained libraries and frameworks. These often include built-in security features and have a community that actively addresses security issues.

Remember that XSS prevention is an ongoing effort. Stay informed about the latest security threats and best practices to ensure your web applications are protected against emerging vulnerabilities.

9.3 Cross-Site Request Forgery (CSRF) Protection

Cross-Site Request Forgery (CSRF) is a security vulnerability where an attacker tricks a user into performing unwanted actions on a different website while they are authenticated on another site. To protect your web application from CSRF attacks, several mitigation techniques can be employed.

Use Anti-CSRF Tokens

One of the most effective ways to prevent CSRF attacks is to use anti-CSRF tokens. These tokens are unique per user session and are included in forms or requests. When a form is submitted, the server verifies that the token is valid, ensuring that the request is legitimate.

Here's an example of how to generate and include an anti-CSRF token in a form using Express.js:

```
const express = require('express');
```

```
const csrf = require('csurf');
```

```javascript
const bodyParser = require('body-parser');

const app = express();

// Use the csrf middleware to generate and validate CSRF tokens

app.use(csrf({ cookie: true }));

app.use(bodyParser.urlencoded({ extended: false }));

// Render a form with the CSRF token

app.get('/form', (req, res) => {

res.render('form', { csrfToken: req.csrfToken() });

});

// Process the form submission and validate the CSRF token

app.post('/submit', (req, res) => {

const submittedToken = req.body._csrf;

if (req.csrfToken() === submittedToken) {

// CSRF token is valid, process the request

// ...

res.send('CSRF protection successful');

} else {

// CSRF token is invalid, reject the request

res.status(403).send('Invalid CSRF token');

}
```

```
});
```

Same-Site Cookies

Setting the SameSite attribute on cookies can help mitigate CSRF attacks. By setting cookies as "SameSite=Strict" or "SameSite=Lax," you limit their scope to the same site, preventing them from being sent in cross-site requests. This is especially effective for cookies that are used for authentication or session management.

```
// Set SameSite attribute for cookies

res.cookie('session', '123456', { sameSite: 'Strict' });
```

Double-Submit Cookies

Double-submit cookies involve generating two tokens: one stored in a cookie and another included in a request parameter. When a request is made, the server compares the two tokens. If they match, the request is considered legitimate.

Here's an example of implementing double-submit cookies in a web application:

```
// Generate and set a double-submit cookie

const doubleSubmitCookie = crypto.randomBytes(16).toString('hex');

res.cookie('doubleSubmitCookie', doubleSubmitCookie);

// Include the double-submit cookie in a request parameter

app.post('/submit', (req, res) => {

const submittedToken = req.body.doubleSubmitCookie;
```

```javascript
if (req.cookies.doubleSubmitCookie === submittedToken) {

// Tokens match, process the request

// ...

res.send('CSRF protection successful');

} else {

// Tokens don't match, reject the request

res.status(403).send('Invalid CSRF token');

}

});
```

These techniques, along with good security practices, can help protect your web application from CSRF attacks. It's crucial to consider security as an integral part of your development process and stay vigilant against emerging threats.

9.4 Content Security Policy (CSP)

Content Security Policy (CSP) is a security feature that helps protect web applications against various types of attacks, including Cross-Site Scripting (XSS) and data injection attacks. CSP allows you to define and enforce a set of rules that dictate which resources, scripts, and content can be loaded and executed on a web page. Implementing CSP can significantly enhance the security of your web application.

Defining a CSP Header

To use CSP, you need to set an HTTP header in your web application's responses. This header specifies the rules for resource loading and script execution. Here's an example of how to set up a basic CSP header in an Express.js application:

```
// Set up Content Security Policy (CSP) header

app.use((req, res, next) => {

res.setHeader('Content-Security-Policy', "default-src 'self'");

next();

});
```

In this example, the default-src 'self' policy allows only resources from the same origin ('self') to be loaded. You can customize this policy to specify trusted sources for scripts, styles, images, fonts, and other types of content.

CSP Directives

CSP allows you to use various directives to specify different types of content and their sources. Here are some common CSP directives:

- default-src: Specifies the default source for content that does not have a specific directive.

- script-src: Defines the sources from which scripts can be loaded and executed.

- style-src: Specifies the sources from which styles (CSS) can be loaded.

- img-src: Defines the sources for images.

- font-src: Specifies the sources for fonts.

- connect-src: Defines the sources for network requests, including AJAX, WebSocket, and Fetch requests.

- media-src: Specifies the sources for audio and video content.

- frame-src: Defines the sources from which frames and iframes can be loaded.

Here's an example of a CSP header with multiple directives:

```
// Set up a comprehensive CSP header

res.setHeader('Content-Security-Policy', `

default-src 'self';

script-src 'self' cdn.example.com;

style-src 'self' fonts.googleapis.com;

img-src 'self' data:;

font-src 'self' fonts.gstatic.com;

connect-src 'self' api.example.com;

media-src 'self' media.example.com;

frame-src 'self' youtube.com;

`);
```

In this example, the CSP header allows scripts from the same origin ('self') and a specific external domain ('cdn.example.com'), styles from the same origin and fonts from 'fonts.googleapis.com,' and so on. You can adjust these directives to suit your application's needs.

Reporting Violations

CSP also allows you to set up reporting to monitor and debug any policy violations. When a violation occurs, the browser can send a report to a specified endpoint. This helps you identify and address potential security issues.

// Set up CSP report-uri

res.setHeader('Content-Security-Policy', "default-src 'self'; report-uri /csp-report-endpoint");

In this example, policy violations will be reported to '/csp-report-endpoint' on your server.

Implementing CSP can be a powerful security measure for your web application. It helps prevent XSS attacks, data injection attacks, and other malicious activities by controlling the sources of content and scripts. Be sure to test your CSP policy thoroughly to ensure it does not unintentionally block legitimate resources.

9.5 Best Practices for Secure Coding

Writing secure JavaScript code is crucial to protect your web applications and users from various security threats. Here are some best practices for secure coding in JavaScript:

1. Input Validation

Always validate user inputs, both on the client and server sides. Input validation prevents malicious data from entering your application and helps protect against SQL injection, Cross-Site Scripting (XSS), and other attacks.

```javascript
// Client-side input validation

const userInput = document.getElementById('user-input').value;

if (!validateInput(userInput)) {

alert('Invalid input!');

}

// Server-side input validation

app.post('/submit', (req, res) => {

const userInput = req.body.input;

if (!validateInput(userInput)) {

res.status(400).send('Invalid input!');

} else {

// Process valid input

}

});
```

2. Avoid Eval

Avoid using the eval() function, as it can execute arbitrary code and is a security risk. Use alternatives like JSON.parse() or other safe parsing methods.

// Avoid eval

const data = JSON.parse(jsonData);

3. Secure Password Handling

When handling passwords, use strong encryption and hashing algorithms, like bcrypt, to store and authenticate user passwords securely.

const bcrypt = require('bcrypt');

// Hashing a password

const password = 'user_password';

const saltRounds = 10;

bcrypt.hash(password, saltRounds, (err, hash) => {

if (err) **throw** err;

// Store hash in the database

});

// Comparing passwords

bcrypt.compare('user_input_password', storedHash, (err, result) =>
{

if (err) **throw** err;

```
if (result) {

// Passwords match

} else {

// Passwords do not match

}

});
```

4. Avoid Storing Sensitive Data in Cookies

Do not store sensitive data, such as passwords or tokens, in cookies. Use secure server-side sessions and tokens for authentication.

5. Regularly Update Dependencies

Keep your JavaScript libraries and dependencies up-to-date to patch security vulnerabilities.

6. Protect Against Cross-Site Request Forgery (CSRF)

Implement anti-CSRF tokens in forms and use the SameSite attribute for cookies to prevent CSRF attacks.

7. Implement Content Security Policy (CSP)

As discussed in the previous section, implement CSP headers to control the sources of scripts and resources, mitigating XSS attacks.

8. Error Handling

Handle errors gracefully and avoid exposing sensitive information in error messages. Use custom error handling and logging to monitor and respond to security issues.

9. Secure APIs

Protect your APIs with authentication and authorization mechanisms, such as API keys, OAuth, or JWT tokens. Validate and sanitize input data to prevent injection attacks.

10. Regular Security Audits

Perform regular security audits and code reviews to identify and address potential vulnerabilities in your JavaScript code.

11. Keep Abreast of Security News

Stay informed about the latest security threats and best practices by following security news, blogs, and community forums.

12. Follow Security Standards

Adhere to industry security standards and guidelines, such as OWASP (Open Web Application Security Project) recommendations, to ensure your application's security.

By following these best practices, you can strengthen the security of your JavaScript applications and reduce the risk of security breaches and data leaks. Remember that security is an ongoing process, and it's essential to stay vigilant and proactive in protecting your applications and users.

Chapter 10: Testing and Debugging

10.1 Unit Testing with Mocha and Chai

Unit testing is a critical aspect of software development that helps ensure the correctness of individual units or functions within your codebase. In JavaScript, Mocha and Chai are popular tools for writing and running unit tests.

What Is Mocha?

Mocha[1] is a flexible JavaScript testing framework that provides a powerful and easy-to-use testing environment. It supports various test styles, including BDD (Behavior-Driven Development) and TDD (Test-Driven Development), and can be used in both the browser and Node.js environments.

Setting Up Mocha

To get started with Mocha, you'll need to install it globally or as a development dependency in your project:

 # Install Mocha globally

npm install -g mocha

 # Install Mocha as a development dependency in your project

npm install—save-dev mocha

Next, create a test directory and add your test files with a .test.js or .spec.js extension. For example, if you have a module named math.js, you can create a corresponding test file named math.test.js.

---

1. https://mochajs.org/

Writing Tests with Mocha

Mocha provides a simple and expressive syntax for defining tests using the describe and it functions. Here's a basic example:

```javascript
const assert = require('assert');

const math = require('./math');

describe('Math module', () => {

it('should add two numbers correctly', () => {

assert.strictEqual(math.add(2, 3), 5);

});

it('should subtract two numbers correctly', () => {

assert.strictEqual(math.subtract(5, 3), 2);

});

});
```

In this example, we're testing a math module with add and subtract functions. The assert module is used for making assertions about the code's behavior.

What Is Chai?

Chai[2] is an assertion library that pairs well with Mocha, providing a more expressive way to make assertions in your tests. It supports different assertion styles, including expect, should, and assert.

---

2. https://www.chaijs.com/

Setting Up Chai

To use Chai with Mocha, you need to install it as a development dependency in your project:

```
npm install—save-dev chai
```

Writing Tests with Chai

Chai allows you to write more human-readable and expressive assertions. Here's an example using the expect style:

```javascript
const math = require('./math');

const expect = require('chai').expect;

describe('Math module', () => {

it('should add two numbers correctly', () => {

expect(math.add(2, 3)).to.equal(5);

});

it('should subtract two numbers correctly', () => {

expect(math.subtract(5, 3)).to.equal(2);

});

});
```

In this example, we're using Chai's expect syntax to make assertions about the results of the add and subtract functions.

Running Tests

To run your Mocha tests, you can use the mocha command followed by the path to your test files or directory:

 # Run tests in the current directory

mocha

 # Run tests in a specific file or directory

mocha tests/

Mocha will execute your tests and provide a clear summary of the results, including any failures or errors.

Unit testing with Mocha and Chai is a fundamental practice for ensuring the reliability and correctness of your JavaScript code. By writing comprehensive tests for your functions and modules, you can catch and fix issues early in the development process, making your code more robust and maintainable.

10.2 Debugging Tools and Techniques

Debugging is an essential skill for any developer, as it helps identify and resolve issues in your code. JavaScript offers various debugging tools and techniques that can streamline the debugging process and make it more efficient.

Browser Developer Tools

Most modern web browsers come equipped with developer tools that provide a range of debugging features. The most commonly used browser developer tools are available in Google Chrome, Mozilla Firefox, Microsoft Edge, and Safari.

Inspecting Elements

You can inspect and modify the HTML and CSS of a web page using the Elements panel in developer tools. This is handy for identifying and fixing layout and styling issues.

Console

The Console panel allows you to view and interact with JavaScript code on a page. You can log messages, errors, and values to the console using console.log(). This is a valuable tool for understanding how your code is behaving and for identifying errors.

Debugger

The Debugger panel enables you to set breakpoints in your JavaScript code, allowing you to pause execution and inspect variables, call stacks, and more. You can step through code execution line by line, making it easier to identify and fix issues.

Network

The Network panel provides insights into network requests made by your web page. This is useful for debugging issues related to API requests, resource loading, and performance optimization.

Node.js Debugger

If you're working with server-side JavaScript using Node.js, you can use the built-in debugging capabilities. Node.js supports debugging through the —inspect flag, which opens a debugging port. You can then connect to this port using tools like the Chrome DevTools or Visual Studio Code for server-side debugging.

Console Methods

The console object in JavaScript offers various methods for debugging:

- console.log(): Outputs a message to the console.

- console.error(): Logs an error message to the console.

- console.warn(): Logs a warning message to the console.

- console.info(): Logs an informational message to the console.

- console.debug(): Logs a debug message to the console (not supported in all browsers).

These methods help you provide context and information about what's happening in your code.

Using debugger Statement

You can insert the debugger statement in your JavaScript code to set a breakpoint. When the code execution reaches the debugger statement, it pauses, and you can inspect variables and step through the code using the browser's developer tools or Node.js debugger.

```javascript
function divide(a, b) {

debugger; // Set a breakpoint here

return a / b;

}

const result = divide(10, 2);
```

console.log(result);

Logging and Error Handling

Strategic use of console.log() statements can help trace the flow of your code and identify issues. Additionally, using try...catch blocks for error handling can prevent your code from breaking entirely when errors occur, allowing for more graceful degradation.

Debugging is an iterative process, and mastering debugging tools and techniques is crucial for becoming a proficient developer. Whether you're working on frontend or backend JavaScript code, having a robust debugging workflow can significantly reduce the time it takes to identify and fix issues.

10.3 Performance Profiling

Performance profiling is the process of analyzing the performance of your JavaScript code to identify bottlenecks and areas for improvement. Profiling helps you optimize your code for better execution speed and resource utilization. In this section, we'll explore various profiling techniques and tools available for JavaScript developers.

Why Is Performance Profiling Important?

Performance is critical in web development because it directly affects user experience. Slow-loading websites and applications can frustrate users and lead to high bounce rates. Therefore, identifying and addressing performance issues is essential.

Profiling Tools

1. **Chrome DevTools**: Google Chrome's developer tools

offer a built-in profiler that can help identify performance bottlenecks in your JavaScript code. You can access it by opening Chrome DevTools, navigating to the "Performance" tab, and clicking the record button to start profiling. After running your code, you'll get a detailed timeline of events, including JavaScript execution, rendering, and more.

2. **Mozilla Firefox Profiler**: Firefox also provides a built-in profiler that's accessible through its developer tools. The profiler can help you analyze JavaScript execution and memory usage. You can capture a profile and analyze it to identify performance issues.

3. **Node.js Profiler**: If you're working with Node.js on the server-side, you can use the built-in profiler. By running your Node.js script with the —inspect flag and using a tool like the Chrome DevTools, you can profile your Node.js code.

Profiling JavaScript Execution

Profiling JavaScript execution helps you understand which parts of your code are consuming the most CPU time. Here's how you can do it using Chrome DevTools:

1. Open Chrome DevTools by right-clicking on your web page, selecting "Inspect," and going to the "Performance" tab.
2. Click the record button to start profiling.
3. Interact with your web page or run the code that you want to profile.
4. Stop profiling by clicking the stop button in Chrome DevTools.
5. Analyze the performance timeline to identify bottlenecks

and areas for improvement.

Profiling Memory Usage

Memory profiling helps you identify memory leaks and excessive memory usage in your JavaScript code. It's essential for maintaining stable web applications. You can use Chrome DevTools for memory profiling:

1. Open Chrome DevTools and go to the "Memory" tab.
2. Click the record button to start memory profiling.
3. Interact with your web page or execute the code you want to profile.
4. Stop memory profiling by clicking the stop button.
5. Analyze the memory snapshot to identify memory-related issues.

Tips for Effective Profiling

- Profiling should be part of your regular development process, not just for debugging performance issues.

- Focus on the most critical parts of your codebase, such as code responsible for rendering or data processing.

- Use profiling tools in both development and production environments to catch issues early and ensure optimal performance in production.

- Address identified bottlenecks and memory issues systematically and retest your code after optimizations.

In summary, performance profiling is a crucial practice for JavaScript developers to ensure their applications run smoothly and efficiently.

Using the right profiling tools and techniques can help you identify and resolve performance bottlenecks and memory issues in your code.

10.4 Continuous Integration and Deployment

Continuous Integration (CI) and Continuous Deployment (CD) are essential practices in modern software development. They automate the process of testing, building, and deploying your JavaScript applications, ensuring that changes are integrated smoothly and deployed to production without manual intervention. In this section, we'll explore the concepts and tools associated with CI/CD in the context of JavaScript development.

Why CI/CD Matters

CI/CD offers several benefits:

1. **Faster Development**: CI/CD pipelines automate repetitive tasks, reducing the time developers spend on manual testing and deployment.
2. **Consistency**: Automated processes ensure that code is tested and deployed consistently, reducing the risk of human error.
3. **Early Issue Detection**: CI/CD pipelines run tests on every code change, allowing for early detection of bugs and issues.
4. **Faster Feedback**: Developers receive quick feedback on the impact of their changes, enabling faster iterations and improvements.
5. **Automated Deployment**: CD automates the deployment process, making it possible to release updates to production

quickly and reliably.

CI/CD Pipeline Components

A typical CI/CD pipeline for a JavaScript project includes the following components:

1. **Source Control**: The code repository, often hosted on platforms like GitHub or GitLab, is where developers collaborate and store code changes.
2. **Build**: The build phase involves compiling, transpiling, and bundling your JavaScript code. Tools like Webpack or Babel are commonly used in this phase.
3. **Testing**: Automated tests, including unit tests, integration tests, and end-to-end tests, are executed to validate the code changes.
4. **Artifact Repository**: Build artifacts, such as compiled JavaScript files or deployment packages, are stored in an artifact repository for later stages.
5. **Deployment**: The deployment phase involves deploying the application to various environments, such as staging and production. Deployment tools like Docker and Kubernetes are used for containerization and orchestration.
6. **Monitoring and Feedback**: Once deployed, monitoring tools collect data about application performance and usage. This feedback loop informs developers about any issues in production.

CI/CD Tools for JavaScript

Several CI/CD tools are popular among JavaScript developers:

- **Jenkins**: An open-source automation server that supports building, deploying, and automating tasks.

- **Travis CI**: A cloud-based CI/CD service that integrates well with GitHub repositories.

- **CircleCI**: A cloud-based CI/CD platform that offers powerful customization options.

- **GitHub Actions**: Integrated directly with GitHub repositories, it allows you to define CI/CD workflows using YAML configuration files.

- **GitLab CI/CD**: Provides CI/CD features within the GitLab platform, offering version control and CI/CD in one place.

Creating a Simple CI/CD Pipeline

Here's a simplified example of a CI/CD pipeline for a JavaScript project:

1. Developers push code changes to a GitHub repository.
2. GitHub Actions, configured with a YAML file, automatically trigger a build and test process whenever changes are pushed.
3. The CI/CD pipeline runs unit tests to ensure code quality.
4. If tests pass, the pipeline deploys the application to a staging environment for further testing.
5. Automated end-to-end tests are run in the staging environment.
6. If all tests pass in the staging environment, the pipeline deploys the application to the production environment.
7. Monitoring tools collect data from the production

environment, providing feedback to developers.

8. If issues arise, the pipeline can be configured to roll back changes or trigger alerts.

In summary, CI/CD is a fundamental practice in modern JavaScript development. It streamlines the process of testing and deploying code changes, leading to faster development cycles, improved code quality, and more reliable production deployments. With the right CI/CD tools and practices, you can automate much of the development workflow and focus on delivering value to your users.

10.5 Code Quality and Code Reviews

Maintaining high code quality is crucial in JavaScript development. Quality code is more maintainable, less error-prone, and easier to collaborate on. In this section, we'll explore the importance of code quality and how code reviews play a vital role in achieving it.

The Importance of Code Quality

Code quality encompasses several aspects, including:

1. **Readability**: Code should be easy for other developers to understand. Clear and consistent formatting, meaningful variable names, and well-structured code contribute to readability.
2. **Maintainability**: High-quality code is easier to maintain and extend. Code should be modular, with well-defined functions and classes that encapsulate specific functionality.
3. **Performance**: Code should be optimized for performance. This includes efficient algorithms and data structures, as well as minimizing resource usage.

4. **Reliability**: Quality code is less likely to contain bugs and vulnerabilities. Testing, error handling, and defensive coding practices are essential for reliability.

5. **Scalability**: Code should be designed to scale as the application grows. Scalable code can handle increased complexity and user load.

Code Reviews

Code reviews involve having other developers examine your code before it is merged into the main codebase. Code reviews offer several benefits:

1. **Error Detection**: Reviewers can catch bugs and issues that the original author might have missed.

2. **Knowledge Sharing**: Code reviews provide an opportunity for knowledge sharing among team members. Reviewers can learn from each other's code.

3. **Coding Standards**: Code reviews enforce coding standards and best practices, ensuring consistency across the codebase.

4. **Quality Assurance**: By requiring code reviews, you establish a quality control process that helps maintain code quality.

5. **Feedback and Improvement**: Reviews provide feedback that helps developers improve their coding skills.

Conducting Code Reviews

When conducting code reviews, consider the following best practices:

1. **Set Clear Expectations**: Define the scope and objectives of the code review. Specify what aspects of the code to

focus on.

2. **Use Code Review Tools**: Utilize code review tools and platforms to streamline the process. Popular tools include GitHub Pull Requests, GitLab Merge Requests, and Bitbucket Code Review.
3. **Focus on the Code, Not the Author**: Emphasize that code reviews are about improving the code, not criticizing the developer. Be respectful and constructive in feedback.
4. **Check for Readability**: Ensure that the code is easy to read and understand. Pay attention to code formatting, comments, and naming conventions.
5. **Test Cases**: Verify that the code includes appropriate test cases to cover different scenarios.
6. **Performance and Efficiency**: Review for any performance bottlenecks or inefficient algorithms.
7. **Security**: Check for security vulnerabilities and adherence to security best practices.
8. **Documentation**: Ensure that code changes are adequately documented.
9. **Consistency**: Ensure that the code adheres to coding standards and style guidelines.
10. **Approval Process**: Define a process for approving code changes, including the number of required approvals and who can approve.

Code Review Workflow

A typical code review workflow involves the following steps:

1. The code author creates a pull request or merge request, requesting a review.
2. One or more reviewers examine the code, providing comments and feedback.

3. The author addresses the feedback, making necessary changes and improvements.
4. Reviewers re-examine the code to ensure all feedback has been addressed.
5. Once approved, the code can be merged into the main codebase.

In summary, code quality is essential for the long-term maintainability and reliability of JavaScript applications. Code reviews are a valuable practice for maintaining and improving code quality by catching errors, enforcing coding standards, and promoting knowledge sharing among team members. Incorporating code reviews into your development process can lead to higher-quality code and a more efficient development workflow.

Chapter 11: Building a Single-Page Application (SPA) 11.1 Introduction to SPAs 11.2 Routing in SPAs 11.3 State Management with Redux 11.4 Building a SPA with React 11.5 SPA Best Practices

Chapter 11: Building a Single-Page Application (SPA)

Section 11.1: Introduction to SPAs

A Single-Page Application (SPA) is a web application or website that interacts with the user by rewriting the current page, rather than loading entire new pages from the server. SPAs provide a more fluid and responsive user experience, similar to that of desktop applications, by dynamically updating content as the user interacts with the application.

Key Characteristics of SPAs

SPAs exhibit several key characteristics that distinguish them from traditional multi-page web applications:

1. **Single HTML Page:** In SPAs, there is typically only one HTML file that serves as the initial entry point. This HTML file contains the structure and layout of the entire application.

2. **Dynamic Content Loading:** SPAs use AJAX (Asynchronous JavaScript and XML) or other techniques to fetch data from the server in the background and update the page content without requiring a full page reload.

3. **Client-Side Routing:** SPAs handle navigation and routing on the client side, allowing different views or components to be displayed based on the URL without requesting new HTML pages from the server.

4. **Smooth Transitions:** SPAs often incorporate smooth transitions and animations between views or components, enhancing the user experience.

5. **State Management:** SPAs maintain application state on the client side, reducing the need for constant server interaction. This enables faster interactions and offline capabilities.

6. **Server as a Data Source:** In SPAs, the server primarily serves as a data source, providing APIs (Application Programming Interfaces) for data retrieval and manipulation, rather than rendering HTML pages.

Advantages of SPAs

Building SPAs offers several advantages:

• **Improved User Experience:** SPAs provide a seamless and responsive user experience, as they can update content without page reloads, resulting in faster interactions.

• **Reduced Server Load:** SPAs offload much of the rendering work to the client side, reducing server load and potentially lowering hosting costs.

• **Support for Offline Mode:** SPAs can store data locally, enabling users to use the application even when they are offline or have a slow internet connection.

• **Easier Maintenance:** With a single-page structure and client-side routing, SPAs are often easier to maintain and scale as the application grows.

• **Rich Interactivity:** SPAs can implement rich interactivity, such as real-time updates and animations, to create engaging user interfaces.

Challenges of SPAs

While SPAs offer many benefits, they also come with some challenges:

- **Initial Load Time:** The initial loading of a SPA can take longer, as all necessary JavaScript and assets must be fetched before rendering.

- **SEO (Search Engine Optimization):** SPAs can face SEO challenges, as search engines may have difficulty indexing dynamic content loaded via JavaScript. Techniques like server-side rendering (SSR) or prerendering can mitigate this issue.

- **Complexity:** SPAs can be more complex to develop than traditional websites, as they require client-side routing, state management, and handling of asynchronous data.

- **Back Button and History:** SPAs must manage browser history and the back button to ensure that users can navigate within the application and maintain a consistent history.

In the following sections, we will delve deeper into the specific aspects of building SPAs, including client-side routing, state management, and best practices for SPA development.

Section 11.2: Routing in SPAs

Routing is a fundamental concept in Single-Page Applications (SPAs) that enables navigation within the application by handling changes in the URL or user interactions. In traditional multi-page web applications, navigation is achieved by requesting different HTML pages from the server. In SPAs, routing is managed on the client side without the need for server requests, resulting in a more dynamic and responsive user experience.

Importance of Client-Side Routing

Client-side routing in SPAs allows developers to map specific URLs or routes to different views or components within the application. This enables users to navigate between different sections of the application without experiencing full page reloads. Key benefits of client-side routing include:

1. **Faster Navigation:** Since only the content that needs to change is fetched and updated, navigation within the SPA is typically faster and smoother.
2. **Better User Experience:** SPAs can provide immediate feedback to user interactions, such as clicking on a navigation link, without waiting for server responses.
3. **Maintained State:** Client-side routing ensures that the state of the application is preserved as users navigate between views, offering a more seamless experience.
4. **Bookmarking and Sharing:** Users can bookmark specific URLs, and those URLs can be shared with others, ensuring that users can return to the same view.

How Client-Side Routing Works

Client-side routing in SPAs relies on JavaScript to intercept URL changes and render the appropriate view or component. Here's how it typically works:

1. **Initialization:** When the SPA loads initially, a JavaScript router library or custom routing code is initialized.

2. **Route Configuration:** Developers define a set of routes, each associated with a specific URL pattern and a corresponding view or component.
3. **Routing Logic:** As the user interacts with the application (e.g., by clicking links or using the browser's back and forward buttons), the router intercepts URL changes.
4. **View Rendering:** When a URL change occurs, the router matches the URL to a defined route and renders the associated view or component without requesting a new HTML page from the server.
5. **Updating the Browser's URL:** The router updates the browser's URL to reflect the current state of the application, ensuring that users can bookmark or share the URL.

Popular JavaScript Routing Libraries

Several JavaScript libraries simplify client-side routing in SPAs. Some popular options include:

• **React Router:** If you're building an application with React, React Router is a widely-used library that provides declarative routing.

• **Vue Router:** Vue.js offers its own routing library, Vue Router, for building SPAs with Vue.js.

• **React Navigation:** When developing mobile apps with React Native, React Navigation is a routing library tailored for mobile navigation patterns.

• **Angular Router:** If you're using Angular, Angular Router is the official routing library that seamlessly integrates with the framework.

Best Practices for SPA Routing

When implementing client-side routing in SPAs, consider the following best practices:

- **Nested Routes:** Organize your routes hierarchically, allowing for nested views and layouts within your application.

- **404 Handling:** Implement a catch-all route or a "Not Found" view to handle unexpected or undefined routes gracefully.

- **Lazy Loading:** Use code splitting and lazy loading to load route-specific JavaScript bundles only when needed, improving initial load times.

- **Route Guards:** Implement route guards to control access to certain routes based on user authentication or authorization.

- **Browser History API:** Utilize the HTML5 History API for clean and user-friendly URLs without hash fragments.

- **Testing:** Write unit tests for your routing logic to ensure that routes and navigation behave as expected.

In the next section, we will explore state management in SPAs, which plays a crucial role in maintaining and sharing data across different views.

Section 11.3: State Management with Redux

State management is a critical aspect of building Single-Page Applications (SPAs) that require the handling and sharing of data between different components and views. Redux is a popular JavaScript library that provides a predictable and centralized way to manage application state in SPAs, especially those built with libraries like React.

The Need for State Management

In SPAs, components often need access to shared data, such as user authentication status, shopping cart contents, or application settings. Without proper state management, passing data between components can become complex and error-prone. Redux addresses these challenges by offering a centralized store to manage application-wide state.

Key Concepts in Redux

Redux is built around a few fundamental concepts:

1. **Store:** The store is a single JavaScript object that represents the entire application state. It is read-only, and changes to the state are made through actions and reducers.
2. **Actions:** Actions are plain JavaScript objects that describe what should change in the application state. They typically have a type property and can carry additional data.
3. **Reducers:** Reducers are pure functions that specify how the application's state should change in response to actions. They take the current state and an action as input and return a new state.
4. **Dispatch:** Dispatching an action is the process of sending an action to the store. It triggers the reducer to update the

state based on the action.

5. **Subscribe:** Components can subscribe to the store to receive updates when the state changes. This allows components to react to changes in the application's data.

Benefits of Using Redux

Redux offers several advantages for state management in SPAs:

- **Predictability:** With Redux, the state changes are predictable and follow a strict pattern, making it easier to understand and debug the application's behavior.

- **Centralization:** All application state is stored in a single location (the store), making it easier to manage and access data across components.

- **Debugging Tools:** Redux provides developer-friendly tools like the Redux DevTools extension, which allows you to inspect and time-travel through state changes.

- **Middleware:** Middleware can be used to add additional functionality to Redux, such as asynchronous actions or logging.

- **Testing:** Since reducers are pure functions, they are easy to test in isolation, ensuring that state changes behave as expected.

Example of Using Redux

Here's a simplified example of how Redux can be used in a React application:

1. **Installation:** First, you need to install the required

packages, including redux and react-redux.

npm install redux react-redux

1. **Store Configuration:** Create a Redux store and configure it with reducers.

```js
// store.js

import { createStore } from 'redux';

import rootReducer from './reducers';

const store = createStore(rootReducer);

export default store;
```

1. **Defining Actions:** Define actions to describe state changes.

```js
// actions.js

export const increment = () => ({ type: 'INCREMENT' });

export const decrement = () => ({ type: 'DECREMENT' });
```

1. **Creating Reducers:** Implement reducers to specify how the state should change in response to actions.

```js
// reducers.js

const counterReducer = (state = 0, action) => {

switch (action.type) {
```

```
case 'INCREMENT':

return state + 1;

case 'DECREMENT':

return state - 1;

default:

return state;

}

};

export default counterReducer;
```

1. **Connecting Components:** Use the connect function from react-redux to connect React components to the Redux store.

```
// Counter.js

import React from 'react';

import { connect } from 'react-redux';

import { increment, decrement } from './actions';

const Counter = ({ count, increment, decrement }) => {

return (

<div>

<p>Count: {count}</p>
```

```jsx
<button onClick={increment}>Increment</button>

<button onClick={decrement}>Decrement</button>

</div>

);

};

const mapStateToProps = (state) => ({

count: state,

});

const mapDispatchToProps = {

increment,

decrement,

};

export default connect(mapStateToProps,
mapDispatchToProps)(Counter);
```

In this example, the Redux store manages the count state, and the Counter component connects to the store to access and update the state using actions.

Conclusion

Redux is a powerful state management library that simplifies the process of managing and sharing data in SPAs. While it may introduce some initial complexity, especially for smaller applications, it becomes highly beneficial as your application grows and requires more sophisticated state management. By adhering to Redux's principles, you can ensure a predictable and maintainable approach to handling application-wide state.

Section 11.4: Building a SPA with React

React is a popular JavaScript library for building user interfaces, and it's widely used in the development of Single-Page Applications (SPAs). In this section, we'll explore how to build a basic SPA using React and its core concepts.

Setting Up a React Project

Before you start building a React SPA, you'll need to set up a development environment. You can create a new React project using a tool called Create React App, which sets up the necessary configuration and dependencies for you. Here are the steps to create a new React project:

1. **Install Node.js:** If you don't have Node.js installed, download and install it from the official website (https://nodejs.org/).
2. **Create a New React Project:** Open your terminal and run the following command to create a new React project using Create React App:

npx create-react-app my-spa

Replace my-spa with your desired project name.

1. **Navigate to the Project Folder:** Change your current directory to the newly created project folder:

cd my-spa

1. **Start the Development Server:** To run your React SPA in development mode, use the following command:

```
npm start
```

This command will start the development server, and you can access your SPA in your web browser at http://localhost:3000.

Creating Components

In React, user interfaces are built by creating reusable components. Components are JavaScript functions or classes that return a piece of the UI. You can create components for different parts of your SPA, such as headers, navigation menus, and content sections. Here's an example of a simple React component:

```
import React from 'react';

function Header() {

return (

<header>

<h1>My SPA</h1>

<nav>

<ul>

<li><a href="/">Home</a></li>

<li><a href="/about">About</a></li>

<li><a href="/contact">Contact</a></li>
```

```
</ul>

</nav>

</header>

);

}
```

export default Header;

Managing Routing

In a SPA, navigation between different sections or pages is typically handled using client-side routing. The react-router-dom library is a popular choice for managing routing in React SPAs. You can install it in your project by running:

npm install react-router-dom

Then, you can set up routing in your SPA like this:

import React **from** 'react';

import { BrowserRouter **as** Router, Route, Switch } **from** 'react-router-dom';

import Header **from** './Header';

import Home **from** './Home';

import About **from** './About';

import Contact **from** './Contact';

function App() {

return (

```
<Router>

<Header />

<main>

<Switch>

<Route path="/" exact component={Home} />

<Route path="/about" component={About} />

<Route path="/contact" component={Contact} />

</Switch>

</main>

</Router>

);

}

export default App;
```

Fetching Data

SPAs often need to fetch data from APIs to display dynamic content. You can use JavaScript's fetch API or libraries like axios to make HTTP requests. Here's an example of fetching data in a React component:

```
import React, { useEffect, useState } from 'react';

function Home() {

const [data, setData] = useState([]);
```

```jsx
useEffect(() => {

fetch('https://api.example.com/data')

.then((response) => response.json())

.then((data) => setData(data))

.catch((error) => console.error('Error fetching data:', error));

}, []);

return (

<div>

<h2>Home Page</h2>

<ul>

{data.map((item) => (

<li key={item.id}>{item.name}</li>

))}

</ul>

</div>

);

}

export default Home;
```

Building and Deployment

To build your React SPA for production, you can use the following command:

npm run build

This command generates optimized production-ready files in the build folder. You can then deploy these files to a web server or hosting platform of your choice.

Conclusion

Building a Single-Page Application with React involves setting up a development environment, creating reusable components, managing routing, and fetching data. React provides a powerful and flexible framework for creating interactive and dynamic user interfaces. As you become more familiar with React and its ecosystem, you can explore advanced topics such as state management with Redux, form handling, and integrating third-party libraries to enhance your SPA.

Section 11.5: SPA Best Practices

When developing Single-Page Applications (SPAs), it's essential to follow best practices to ensure that your application is performant, maintainable, and user-friendly. In this section, we'll discuss some key best practices for building and optimizing SPAs.

1. Code Splitting

- **Lazy Loading**: Implement lazy loading for your SPA's modules or routes. This means that you load code only when it's needed, reducing the initial page load time. You can use tools like React's React.lazy() or dynamic import() in modern JavaScript.

```javascript
// Example of lazy loading a component in React

const MyLazyComponent = React.lazy(() => import('./MyLazyComponent'));
```

2. Optimizing Bundle Size

- **Tree Shaking**: Use tree shaking to eliminate unused code from your JavaScript bundles. This can significantly reduce the bundle size.

- **Code Splitting**: Split your application into smaller bundles, especially if it's large. Webpack and tools like react-loadable can help with this.

```javascript
// Example of code splitting in Webpack

import(/* webpackChunkName: "my-chunk-name" */ './MyComponent').then((module) => {

const MyComponent = module.default;

// Use MyComponent...

});
```

3. Minification and Compression

- **Minify Code**: Minify your JavaScript, HTML, and CSS files in production to remove unnecessary whitespace and reduce file size.

- **Compression**: Enable gzip or Brotli compression on your web server to further reduce file sizes when serving them to clients.

4. Client-Side Routing

- **Use a Router Library**: Utilize a routing library like react-router to handle client-side routing efficiently.

- **Fallback Routes**: Implement a catch-all or fallback route that directs users to a not-found page if they access an undefined route.

// Example of a fallback route in React Router

```
<Route component={NotFoundPage} />
```

5. Optimized Images and Assets

- **Image Compression**: Optimize and compress images before including them in your SPA. Use modern image formats like WebP for better compression.

- **Responsive Images**: Implement responsive images to serve different sizes based on the user's device and screen resolution.

6. Caching Strategies

- **Caching**: Implement caching strategies for assets, API responses, and other resources using Service Workers or browser caching mechanisms.

7. Error Handling

- **Graceful Error Handling**: Implement error boundaries in your SPA to gracefully handle and display errors without crashing the entire application.

```
// Example of an error boundary in React

class ErrorBoundary extends React.Component {

componentDidCatch(error, errorInfo) {

// Log error information or send it to a logging service

}

render() {

if (this.state.hasError) {

return <ErrorFallbackComponent />;

}

return this.props.children;

}

}
```

8. Progressive Web App (PWA) Features

- **PWA Enhancements**: If applicable, consider adding PWA features like offline support, background sync, and push notifications to improve the user experience.

9. Security Considerations

- **Security Headers**: Implement security headers such as Content Security Policy (CSP) to protect your SPA against cross-site scripting (XSS) and other security threats.

- **Authentication**: Secure user authentication and authorization, especially if your SPA relies on user-specific data.

10. Testing and Performance Monitoring

- **Testing**: Continuously test your SPA for performance using tools like Lighthouse, WebPageTest, or Google PageSpeed Insights.

- **Monitoring**: Implement performance monitoring and error tracking to identify and address issues in real-time.

Following these best practices will help you create a robust and user-friendly SPA that provides a smooth experience for your users while optimizing performance and maintainability. Remember that SPAs require careful attention to performance and user experience due to their dynamic nature, and regular optimization is key to success.

Chapter 12: Mobile App Development with JavaScript

Section 12.1: Overview of Mobile App Development

Mobile app development has become an integral part of the digital landscape, and JavaScript plays a significant role in this domain. In this section, we will provide an overview of mobile app development using JavaScript, focusing on various approaches and technologies.

The Mobile App Landscape

Mobile apps are software applications specifically designed to run on mobile devices such as smartphones and tablets. They offer a wide range of functionalities, from productivity tools and social networking to gaming and multimedia experiences. The mobile app market has seen explosive growth, making it a lucrative space for developers.

JavaScript in Mobile App Development

JavaScript has evolved into a versatile language that can be used for building cross-platform mobile apps. Developers can leverage their existing JavaScript skills to create mobile apps for different platforms, including iOS and Android. There are several frameworks and tools available to facilitate JavaScript-based mobile app development:

1. **React Native**: Developed by Facebook, React Native allows you to build native mobile apps using React and JavaScript. It offers a component-based architecture and allows for code reuse between iOS and Android.

2. **Ionic Framework**: Ionic is an open-source framework for building cross-platform mobile apps using web technologies like HTML, CSS, and JavaScript. It provides a set of UI components and integrates with Angular or React.

3. **Apache Cordova**: Cordova, formerly known as PhoneGap, enables you to build mobile apps using HTML, CSS, and JavaScript. It provides access to native device features through plugins, making it a versatile choice.

4. **Flutter**: While not based on JavaScript, Flutter is a popular

cross-platform framework developed by Google that uses the Dart programming language. It allows for high-quality, natively compiled apps for mobile, web, and desktop from a single codebase.

Advantages of JavaScript-Based Mobile Development

JavaScript-based mobile development offers several advantages:

- **Code Reusability**: You can reuse a significant portion of your codebase when targeting multiple platforms, saving development time and effort.

- **Access to Native Features**: Frameworks like React Native and Apache Cordova provide access to native device features, such as the camera, GPS, and sensors.

- **Large Developer Community**: JavaScript has a vast and active developer community, providing ample resources and support for mobile app developers.

- **Cost-Effective**: Using JavaScript for mobile development can be more cost-effective than hiring separate teams for iOS and Android development.

- **Rapid Development**: JavaScript frameworks often allow for rapid development and hot-reloading, making the development process more efficient.

However, it's essential to consider the specific needs of your project when choosing a JavaScript-based framework for mobile app development. Each framework has its strengths and weaknesses, and the choice may depend on factors such as project complexity, team expertise, and performance requirements.

In the following sections of this chapter, we will explore specific JavaScript frameworks and tools for mobile app development in more detail, providing insights into their features, use cases, and best practices. Whether you are a web developer looking to expand into mobile app development or a seasoned mobile app developer exploring JavaScript-based solutions, this chapter will equip you with valuable knowledge to embark on your mobile app development journey.

Section 12.2: React Native for Cross-Platform Apps

React Native is a popular JavaScript framework developed by Facebook for building cross-platform mobile applications. It allows developers to create native mobile apps for iOS, Android, and even other platforms from a single codebase. React Native leverages the React library, which is widely used for web development, and extends it to mobile development.

Key Features of React Native

1. **Native-Like Performance**: React Native apps provide a near-native performance experience, thanks to the use of native components and optimization techniques.
2. **Code Reusability**: With React Native, a significant portion of code can be shared between iOS and Android, reducing development effort.
3. **Hot Reloading**: Developers can see the results of their changes almost instantly with hot reloading, speeding up the development process.
4. **Rich Ecosystem**: React Native has a vast ecosystem of libraries, components, and plugins contributed by the community, making it easy to integrate various

functionalities into your app.

5. **React-Style Development**: If you're already familiar with React, transitioning to React Native is relatively seamless, as it follows a similar component-based architecture.
6. **Access to Native Modules**: You can access native modules and APIs using React Native, enabling interactions with device-specific features like camera, GPS, and sensors.

Getting Started with React Native

To get started with React Native, you need to have Node.js and npm (Node Package Manager) installed on your machine. Follow these steps:

1. **Install Node.js and npm**: Download and install Node.js from the official website (https://nodejs.org/), which includes npm.
2. **Install Expo CLI (optional)**: Expo is a set of tools and services that makes it easier to build React Native apps. You can install the Expo CLI globally using npm: npm install -g expo-cli.
3. **Create a New React Native Project**: You can create a new React Native project using the following command:

npx react-native init MyApp

Replace MyApp with the name of your project.

1. **Run Your Project**: Navigate to your project's directory and start the development server:

cd MyApp

npx react-native start

You can run your app on an iOS or Android emulator, or on a physical device, depending on your setup. The commands to start the app on different platforms are provided in the project's documentation.

Building Your First React Native App

A simple "Hello World" example in React Native looks like this:

```javascript
import React from 'react';

import { View, Text, StyleSheet } from 'react-native';

const App = () => {

return (

<View style={styles.container}>

<Text>Hello, React Native!</Text>

</View>

);

};

const styles = StyleSheet.create({

container: {

flex: 1,

justifyContent: 'center',

alignItems: 'center',

},
```

```
});
```

export default App;

In this example, we import necessary components from react-native, define a functional component App, and render a simple "Hello, React Native!" message inside a View component. The StyleSheet is used to define styles for the components.

You can run this app on an emulator or device to see the result.

Conclusion

React Native is a powerful and versatile framework for building cross-platform mobile apps using JavaScript. It offers native-like performance, code reusability, and a rich ecosystem of libraries and components. In the next sections, we will explore more advanced topics and best practices for React Native development, helping you create high-quality mobile applications.

Section 12.3: Ionic Framework for Hybrid Apps

Ionic is a popular open-source framework for building hybrid mobile applications using web technologies such as HTML, CSS, and JavaScript. Hybrid apps are web apps that are wrapped in a native container, allowing them to run on multiple platforms like iOS, Android, and the web, using a single codebase. Ionic provides a wide range of UI components and tools to simplify the development process and create visually appealing, cross-platform mobile apps.

Key Features of Ionic Framework

1. **Cross-Platform Development**: Ionic enables developers

to write code once and deploy it on multiple platforms, reducing development time and effort.

2. **Native-Like UI**: Ionic offers a library of pre-designed UI components and themes that provide a native-like look and feel to your app.

3. **Access to Device Features**: You can access native device features and APIs using plugins, allowing you to interact with device hardware like the camera, GPS, and more.

4. **Rich Ecosystem**: Ionic has a vibrant ecosystem of plugins and extensions, which can be easily integrated into your app to add functionality.

5. **Cordova Integration**: Ionic integrates seamlessly with Apache Cordova, a platform for building native mobile applications using web technologies, giving you access to a wide range of native APIs.

6. **Live Reload**: You can see your changes in real-time with live reload, making development faster and more efficient.

Getting Started with Ionic

To get started with Ionic, follow these steps:

1. **Install Node.js and npm**: Similar to React Native, you need to have Node.js and npm installed on your machine. You can download them from the official website (https://nodejs.org/).

2. **Install Ionic CLI**: Install the Ionic Command Line Interface (CLI) globally using npm:

```
npm install -g @ionic/cli
```

1. **Create a New Ionic App**: You can create a new Ionic app using the following command:

```
ionic start myApp blank
```

Replace myApp with the name of your project and blank with the starter template of your choice. Ionic provides several starter templates catering to different types of apps.

1. **Run Your App**: Navigate to your project's directory and run your app in a web browser:

```
cd myApp
```

```
ionic serve
```

This will open your app in a web browser, allowing you to test it during development.

Building Your First Ionic App

Here's a simple example of creating a "Hello World" app in Ionic:

1. Navigate to your project's directory and open the src/app/home/home.page.html file.
2. Replace the content with the following HTML code:

```html
<ion-header [translucent]="true">

<ion-toolbar>

<ion-title>

Hello, Ionic!

</ion-title>

</ion-toolbar>
```

```
</ion-header>

<ion-content [fullscreen]="true">

<ion-header collapse="condense">

<ion-toolbar>

<ion-title size="large">Hello, Ionic!</ion-title>

</ion-toolbar>

</ion-header>

<div class="ion-padding">

The world of hybrid mobile apps awaits you.

</div>

</ion-content>
```

1. Save the file, and you'll see the changes reflected in the
    browser automatically.

Conclusion

Ionic is a powerful framework for building hybrid mobile apps using
web technologies. It provides a wide range of UI components,
plugins, and tools to streamline the development process. Whether
you're targeting iOS, Android, or the web, Ionic offers a consistent
and visually appealing user experience. In the next sections, we'll
explore advanced topics and best practices for Ionic development,
helping you create high-quality hybrid mobile applications.

Section 12.4: PWA: Progressive Web Apps

Progressive Web Apps (PWAs) are a modern approach to web development that combines the best of both web and mobile app experiences. They are web applications that can be accessed through web browsers but offer a native app-like experience with features such as offline access, push notifications, and fast loading times. PWAs have gained popularity for their ability to work across various platforms and devices while providing a consistent user experience.

Key Features of PWAs

1. **Offline Access**: PWAs use service workers, a type of JavaScript worker, to cache resources and enable offline access. Users can continue using the app even when they are not connected to the internet.
2. **Responsive Design**: PWAs are designed to adapt to different screen sizes and orientations, making them suitable for both desktop and mobile devices.
3. **Fast Loading**: Service workers can cache assets and content, leading to faster loading times, especially on repeat visits.
4. **App-Like Experience**: PWAs offer a user experience similar to native mobile apps, with smooth animations, gestures, and a home screen icon for quick access.
5. **Push Notifications**: PWAs can send push notifications to users, keeping them engaged and informed even when the app is not open.
6. **Improved Security**: PWAs are served over HTTPS, ensuring data security and user privacy.

Building a PWA

To create a PWA, follow these general steps:

1. **Create a Web App**: Start by building a web application using HTML, CSS, and JavaScript. Ensure your site is responsive and optimized for mobile devices.

2. **Implement Service Workers**: Service workers are at the core of PWAs. They are JavaScript files that run in the background, intercept network requests, and manage caching. Implement service workers to enable offline access and faster loading times.

3. **Add a Manifest File**: Create a manifest file (usually manifest.json) that provides metadata about your PWA, such as its name, icons, and theme colors. This file helps browsers understand how to display and launch your app.

4. **Ensure HTTPS**: PWAs must be served over HTTPS to ensure data security and allow the use of service workers.

5. **Testing**: Test your PWA thoroughly, especially its offline capabilities and responsiveness on various devices.

6. **Install Prompt**: Implement an install prompt that encourages users to add your PWA to their home screens. This is done through a browser-provided API.

7. **Push Notifications**: If your app requires push notifications, implement the necessary code to handle them.

8. **Deployment**: Host your PWA on a web server or a hosting platform. Ensure that your server supports HTTPS.

PWA Examples

Several well-known companies have adopted PWAs to enhance their web experiences:

- **Twitter Lite**: Twitter's PWA offers a similar experience to its native app, including offline access and push notifications.

- **Pinterest**: Pinterest's PWA allows users to browse and save pins even when they are offline.

- **Uber**: Uber's PWA provides a streamlined booking experience and loads quickly, even on slow networks.

- **Flipkart**: Flipkart's PWA offers an app-like shopping experience with fast loading times and the ability to add a shortcut to the home screen.

Conclusion

Progressive Web Apps provide an exciting way to deliver web content with a native app-like experience. They offer offline access, fast loading times, and the ability to engage users through push notifications. By following best practices and leveraging modern web technologies, you can create PWAs that offer a compelling and consistent experience across various platforms and devices. In the next section, we'll explore the deployment and distribution of PWAs, ensuring that your users can easily access and install your app.

Section 12.5: App Store Deployment

Once you've developed a mobile app using JavaScript, whether it's a native app created with a framework like React Native or a Progressive Web App (PWA), you might want to distribute it through app stores like the Apple App Store and Google Play Store. This section will guide you through the process of preparing your app for app store deployment and submitting it for review.

Native App Deployment

1. Code Signing and Building: For native apps, you'll need to set up code signing for both iOS (Apple) and Android (Google Play). This involves creating and configuring certificates and provisioning profiles for iOS and keystore files for Android. Once set up, build your app for each platform.

2. App Store Developer Accounts: To publish your app on the Apple App Store, you need an Apple Developer account. For the Google Play Store, you need a Google Play Console account. These accounts require a one-time registration fee.

3. App Submission: Prepare the assets and information required for app store submission, including app icons, screenshots, descriptions, and privacy policy URLs. Follow the respective guidelines for each app store.

4. App Review: Submit your app for review. Apple and Google will review your app to ensure it complies with their guidelines and policies. This process can take several days to weeks.

5. Release and Updates: Once your app is approved, you can choose to release it immediately or schedule a release date. You can also release updates to your app to provide new features or fix issues.

PWA Deployment

1. PWA Manifest: Ensure your PWA has a valid manifest file (usually manifest.json) that includes information like the app's name, icons, and theme colors. This helps browsers understand how to present your PWA to users.

2. HTTPS Hosting: PWAs must be served over HTTPS to ensure data security. Use a web hosting service that supports HTTPS, or set up SSL/TLS certificates for your server.

3. Service Workers: Make sure your service workers are correctly implemented to enable features like offline access and caching. Test your PWA thoroughly, especially its offline capabilities.

4. Add to Home Screen: Implement a prompt that encourages users to add your PWA to their device's home screen. This can be achieved using the browser's built-in Add to Home Screen functionality.

Distribution Considerations

1. User Acquisition: Promote your app or PWA to acquire users. This can include marketing, social media promotion, and app store optimization (ASO) to improve visibility in app stores.

2. User Feedback: Encourage users to provide feedback and ratings on the app stores. Positive reviews can improve your app's visibility.

3. Maintenance and Updates: Continuously maintain and update your app or PWA to fix bugs, add new features, and ensure compatibility with the latest devices and operating systems.

4. Analytics: Use analytics tools to gather data on user behavior, app usage, and performance. This data can help you make informed decisions for future updates.

5. *App Store Guidelines: Stay informed about changes in app store guidelines and policies, as non-compliance can lead to removal from the app stores.*

Conclusion

Deploying your JavaScript-based mobile app or PWA to app stores is a significant step in reaching a broader audience. Whether you choose to publish a native app or leverage the capabilities of PWAs, it's essential to follow best practices, ensure compliance with store guidelines, and actively engage with users to provide a positive app experience. Remember that the deployment process may differ slightly for iOS and Android, so consult the respective documentation for detailed instructions.

Chapter 13: Web Performance Optimization

Section 13.1: Understanding Web Performance

Web performance optimization is a critical aspect of web development. A fast and responsive web application not only provides a better user experience but also positively impacts search engine rankings and user engagement. In this section, we'll delve into the fundamentals of web performance, explore why it matters, and discuss the key metrics and tools used for performance analysis.

Why Web Performance Matters

1. **User Experience**: Faster websites and web applications are more enjoyable to use. Users are more likely to stay engaged and convert when they don't have to wait for pages to load.
2. **Search Engine Ranking**: Search engines like Google consider page speed as a ranking factor. Faster websites tend to rank higher in search results, increasing their visibility.
3. **Mobile Devices**: With the increasing use of mobile devices, optimizing for performance is crucial. Mobile users often have slower internet connections and limited processing power, making performance even more critical.
4. **Conversion Rates**: Improved performance can lead to higher conversion rates, whether you're selling products, collecting leads, or aiming for any other user interaction.

Key Performance Metrics

To assess web performance, you need to measure various metrics:

1. **Page Load Time**: This is the time it takes for a page to fully load in the user's browser. It includes the time for HTML, CSS, JavaScript, images, and other assets to load and render.
2. **First Contentful Paint (FCP)**: FCP measures when the first content (text, images, etc.) appears on the screen. It indicates that the page is actively loading.
3. **Time to Interactive (TTI)**: TTI measures when a page becomes interactive and responsive to user input. It's a critical metric for user experience.
4. **Total Blocking Time (TBT)**: TBT calculates the time during which the main thread is blocked by long tasks, potentially affecting interactivity.
5. **Cumulative Layout Shift (CLS)**: CLS measures unexpected layout shifts that can be disruptive to users, such as when an element moves as they're trying to interact with it.

Tools for Performance Analysis

Several tools can help you analyze and optimize web performance:

1. **Google PageSpeed Insights**: This tool provides a performance score for your website and offers suggestions for improvement.
2. **Lighthouse**: Integrated into Chrome DevTools, Lighthouse offers detailed performance audits and recommendations for web pages.
3. **WebPageTest**: This online tool allows you to test your website's performance from different locations and devices,

providing a comprehensive performance report.

4. **GTmetrix**: GTmetrix analyzes your page's speed performance and provides actionable recommendations to optimize it.
5. **Browser DevTools**: Browsers like Chrome and Firefox offer built-in developer tools with performance analysis features, including network throttling and timeline recordings.

Conclusion

Web performance is a critical aspect of web development that affects user experience, search engine rankings, and business outcomes. Understanding key performance metrics and using performance analysis tools is essential for optimizing your web applications and ensuring they provide a fast and responsive experience for users. In the following sections, we'll explore specific techniques and strategies for improving web performance.

Section 13.2: Loading and Rendering Optimization

Optimizing loading and rendering performance is crucial for ensuring that web pages appear quickly and smoothly to users. In this section, we will explore various techniques and best practices to enhance the loading and rendering performance of your web applications.

Lazy Loading of Images

One effective technique for improving page loading speed is lazy loading images. With lazy loading, images are loaded only when they enter the viewport, reducing initial page load time. HTML attributes such as loading="lazy" can be used to implement this feature:

```
<img src="image.jpg" alt="Lazy-loaded image" loading="lazy">
```

Modern browsers support lazy loading natively, making it easy to implement.

Minification and Compression

Minifying and compressing your HTML, CSS, and JavaScript files can significantly reduce file sizes, leading to faster page loading times. Minification removes unnecessary characters and whitespace, while compression (e.g., GZIP) reduces the size of files during transmission. Many build tools and online services can automate this process.

Content Delivery Networks (CDNs)

CDNs are distributed networks of servers that cache and deliver web content from locations closer to users. By leveraging CDNs, you can reduce the distance data needs to travel, improving loading times for users around the world. Popular CDNs include Cloudflare, Akamai, and Amazon CloudFront.

Browser Caching

Leveraging browser caching allows you to store static assets like images, stylesheets, and scripts in the user's browser cache. When a user revisits your website, these assets can be loaded from the cache, reducing the need for re-downloading. You can set cache-control headers on your server to control how long assets are cached.

Critical Rendering Path Optimization

The critical rendering path refers to the sequence of steps a browser takes to render a web page. Optimizing this path is essential for fast rendering. Some key optimizations include:

- **Minimizing Render-Blocking Resources**: Reduce the number of external stylesheets and scripts that block rendering. Use async or defer attributes for scripts when appropriate.

- **Inline Critical CSS**: Include critical CSS directly in the HTML to reduce the time to first render. Tools like CriticalCSS can automate this process.

- **Responsive Images**: Use responsive image techniques like srcset and sizes attributes to serve appropriately sized images based on the user's device and viewport.

- **Optimize Fonts**: Minimize the use of custom fonts and consider using system fonts to speed up rendering.

Preloading and Prefetching

Preloading and prefetching allow you to instruct the browser to load certain resources in the background, improving perceived performance. For example, you can preload critical CSS or prefetch linked pages that the user might navigate to. Here's an example of prefetching:

```html
<link rel="prefetch" href="next-page.html">
```

Conclusion

Loading and rendering optimization techniques play a vital role in ensuring that web pages load quickly and provide a smooth user experience. By implementing lazy loading, minification, leveraging CDNs, optimizing caching, and optimizing the critical rendering path, you can significantly enhance the performance of your web applications. These strategies are essential for keeping users engaged and satisfied with your website. In the next section, we will explore network and server-side optimization techniques.

Section 13.3: Network and Server-Side Optimization

Network and server-side optimization is critical for improving the performance of web applications by reducing latency and enhancing the overall user experience. In this section, we'll explore various strategies and techniques to optimize the network and server-side aspects of web development.

Content Delivery Networks (CDNs)

Content Delivery Networks (CDNs) were briefly mentioned in the previous section, but they deserve further attention. CDNs play a vital role in network optimization by distributing website content to multiple servers strategically placed around the world. When a user requests your website, the CDN serves content from the nearest server, reducing the time it takes for data to travel and load. Popular CDNs include Cloudflare, Akamai, and Amazon CloudFront.

HTTP/2 and HTTP/3

Upgrading to the latest versions of the HTTP protocol, such as HTTP/2 and HTTP/3, can significantly improve network performance. These protocols introduce features like multiplexing, header compression, and prioritization, which reduce latency and speed up the loading of web pages. Many web servers and browsers support HTTP/2 and HTTP/3, making it feasible to adopt them in your web applications.

Resource Bundling and Code Splitting

Combining multiple CSS or JavaScript files into bundles reduces the number of requests made to the server, improving loading times. However, large bundles can delay initial page rendering. Code splitting is a technique that breaks code into smaller, more manageable pieces, allowing you to load only the necessary code for a specific page or feature. This can result in faster loading times for critical content.

Server-Side Rendering (SSR) and Static Site Generation (SSG)

Server-Side Rendering (SSR) and Static Site Generation (SSG) are techniques that improve server-side optimization. SSR generates HTML on the server and sends a fully rendered page to the client, reducing client-side rendering time. SSG pre-builds HTML pages during the build process, resulting in faster loading times. Popular frameworks like Next.js and Nuxt.js simplify SSR and SSG implementations.

Content Compression

Compressing content before sending it to the client can significantly reduce file sizes and decrease load times. Techniques like GZIP and Brotli compression can be applied to HTML, CSS, JavaScript, and other assets. Most web servers support content compression, and it's relatively easy to configure.

Efficient Database Queries

Efficiently querying databases is crucial for server-side optimization. Use indexes, pagination, and caching to minimize the impact of database queries on server performance. Additionally, consider using NoSQL databases or caching layers to offload read-heavy operations.

Server-Side Caching

Implementing server-side caching can dramatically reduce server load and response times. Use tools like Redis or Memcached for caching frequently accessed data or HTML fragments. Popular content management systems (CMS) and web frameworks offer caching mechanisms.

Conclusion

Network and server-side optimization are essential components of web performance. By leveraging CDNs, adopting modern HTTP protocols, optimizing resource delivery, implementing SSR and SSG, compressing content, and efficiently managing databases and caching, you can significantly enhance the speed and responsiveness of your web applications. These optimizations contribute to a better user experience and can positively impact your website's search engine ranking. In the next section, we'll delve into caching and compression techniques.

Section 13.4: Caching and Compression Techniques

Caching and compression are fundamental techniques in web performance optimization. They help reduce load times, improve user experience, and minimize bandwidth usage. In this section, we'll explore various caching and compression techniques used in web development.

Browser Caching

Browser caching allows web browsers to store copies of static assets like images, stylesheets, and scripts locally. When a user revisits your website, their browser can retrieve these assets from its cache, reducing the need to re-download them from the server. To enable browser caching, you can set appropriate HTTP headers in your server's response, specifying how long assets should be cached.

Here's an example of HTTP headers to enable browser caching for one year:

Cache-Control: public, max-age=31536000

Expires: [current date + 1 year]

Server-Side Caching

Server-side caching involves storing the generated HTML or data on the server so that it can be quickly served to subsequent users without re-computation. Popular tools like Redis, Memcached, and Varnish are used for server-side caching.

For instance, in a Content Management System (CMS), you can cache the rendered HTML of frequently accessed pages. When a user requests the same page, the cached HTML is delivered, reducing server load and improving response times.

Content Compression

Compressing content before sending it to the client can significantly reduce file sizes and load times. Two common compression methods are GZIP and Brotli.

GZIP Compression

GZIP is a widely supported compression method that reduces the size of text-based assets like HTML, CSS, and JavaScript. Web servers can be configured to compress responses using GZIP, and browsers automatically decompress these files upon receipt.

Here's an example of enabling GZIP compression in an Apache server's configuration:

```
<IfModule mod_deflate.c>

AddOutputFilterByType DEFLATE text/html text/plain text/xml text/css text/javascript application/javascript application/x-javascript application/json application/xml

</IfModule>
```

Brotli Compression

Brotli is a newer compression algorithm developed by Google. It typically provides better compression ratios than GZIP, resulting in smaller file sizes and faster downloads. Brotli is supported by modern browsers and web servers.

To enable Brotli compression in Nginx, you can use the following configuration:

```
gzip on;
```

gzip_static on;

gzip_proxied any;

gzip_types text/plain text/css text/xml text/javascript application/javascript application/json application/xml+rss;

Image Compression

Images often contribute significantly to page load times. You can optimize images by compressing them without noticeable loss of quality. Tools like ImageOptim, TinyPNG, and ImageMagick can help reduce image file sizes.

Conclusion

Caching and compression techniques are essential for improving web performance. By leveraging browser caching, implementing server-side caching, and compressing content using methods like GZIP and Brotli, you can enhance the speed and responsiveness of your web applications. Additionally, optimizing images can further reduce load times, resulting in a better user experience. In the next section, we'll explore methods for measuring and monitoring performance.

Section 13.5: Measuring and Monitoring Performance

Measuring and monitoring the performance of your web applications is crucial to ensure they deliver a smooth and efficient user experience. In this section, we'll explore various tools and techniques for measuring and monitoring web performance.

Performance Metrics

Before optimizing performance, you need to understand the key performance metrics that impact user experience:

1. **Page Load Time**: The time it takes for a web page to load completely in the user's browser.
2. **Time to First Byte (TTFB)**: The time it takes for the first byte of data to be received from the server after the user requests a web page.
3. **First Contentful Paint (FCP)**: The time it takes for the browser to render the first piece of content on the screen, such as text or an image.
4. **Time to Interactive (TTI)**: The time it takes for a web page to become fully interactive and responsive to user input.
5. **Total Blocking Time (TBT)**: The cumulative amount of time during which the main thread is blocked and cannot respond to user input.
6. **Largest Contentful Paint (LCP)**: The time it takes for the largest content element (e.g., an image or text block) to become visible within the viewport.
7. **Cumulative Layout Shift (CLS)**: A measure of how much the content layout shifts during loading, which can be annoying to users.

Web Performance Tools

There are several tools available to measure and monitor web performance:

Google PageSpeed Insights

Google PageSpeed Insights[1] analyzes web pages and provides performance scores along with optimization suggestions. It also offers a field data report based on real user experiences.

Lighthouse

Lighthouse[2] is an open-source tool from Google that audits web pages for performance, accessibility, SEO, and more. It's available as a browser extension and through the Chrome DevTools.

WebPagetest

WebPagetest[3] is an online tool that allows you to test the performance of your web pages from multiple locations and browsers. It provides detailed waterfall charts and performance metrics.

GTmetrix

GTmetrix[4] is another online tool that analyzes your web page's performance and suggests optimizations. It provides scores based on Google's PageSpeed and Yahoo's YSlow rules.

Real User Monitoring (RUM)

Real User Monitoring involves collecting data from actual users of your website. Services like New Relic[5] and Datadog[6] offer RUM

---

1. https://developers.google.com/speed/pagespeed/insights

2. https://developers.google.com/web/tools/lighthouse

3. https://www.webpagetest.org/

4. https://gtmetrix.com/

solutions that allow you to track performance metrics, user interactions, and error rates in real-time.

Synthetic Monitoring

Synthetic monitoring involves simulating user interactions and monitoring performance under controlled conditions. Tools like Pingdom[7] and SpeedCurve[8] provide synthetic monitoring capabilities.

Continuous Integration and Deployment (CI/CD) Integration

Integrate performance testing into your CI/CD pipeline to catch performance regressions early. Tools like Lighthouse CI[9] and Sitespeed.io[10] can be used for automated performance testing.

Conclusion

Measuring and monitoring web performance is an ongoing process that helps you identify bottlenecks and deliver a better user experience. By understanding key performance metrics and utilizing tools like Google PageSpeed Insights, Lighthouse, WebPagetest, and real user monitoring solutions, you can optimize your web applications for speed and responsiveness. Additionally, integrating performance testing into your CI/CD pipeline ensures that performance remains a top priority throughout your development

---

5. https://newrelic.com/

6. https://www.datadog.com/

7. https://www.pingdom.com/

8. https://speedcurve.com/

9. https://github.com/GoogleChrome/lighthouse-ci

10. https://www.sitespeed.io/

process. In the next chapter, we'll delve into JavaScript's role in web accessibility.

Chapter 14: JavaScript and Accessibility

Section 14.1: Web Accessibility Principles

Web accessibility is the practice of making web content and applications usable by people with disabilities. It ensures that everyone, regardless of their abilities or disabilities, can perceive, navigate, and interact with web content effectively. Web accessibility is not only a legal requirement in many countries but also a fundamental aspect of creating inclusive and user-friendly websites and web applications.

Why Web Accessibility Matters

Web accessibility matters for several reasons:

1. **Inclusivity**: Accessibility ensures that your digital products are usable by the widest possible audience, including people with disabilities.
2. **Legal Compliance**: Many countries and regions have laws and regulations requiring web accessibility. Non-compliance can lead to legal consequences.
3. **Improved User Experience**: Making your web content accessible often results in a better user experience for everyone, not just those with disabilities.
4. **SEO Benefits**: Accessible websites tend to perform better in search engine rankings, as search engines value semantic HTML and well-structured content.

Key Accessibility Principles

To create accessible web content, you should follow these key principles:

1. **Perceivable**: Information and user interface components must be presented in ways that users can perceive. This includes providing text alternatives for non-text content (e.g., images), using captions and transcripts for multimedia, and ensuring that content is adaptable and distinguishable.
2. **Operable**: Users must be able to interact with web content and navigate it effectively. This means ensuring keyboard accessibility, providing logical and consistent navigation, and avoiding content that may cause seizures or physical discomfort.
3. **Understandable**: Web content should be clear and easy to understand. Use plain language, provide clear instructions, and ensure predictable and consistent navigation and functionality.
4. **Robust**: Web content should be compatible with current and future technologies, including assistive technologies. Use valid and semantic HTML, provide ARIA (Accessible Rich Internet Applications) roles and attributes where necessary, and avoid reliance on specific technologies or presentation methods.

Assistive Technologies

Assistive technologies, such as screen readers, braille displays, voice recognition software, and switches, help people with disabilities interact with digital content. Web developers should ensure that their websites and web applications are compatible with these tools by following accessibility guidelines.

Accessibility Testing

To ensure web accessibility, consider using tools like automated accessibility checkers (e.g., Axe, WAVE, or aXe-core) and conducting manual testing with assistive technologies. Regular accessibility audits and user testing involving people with disabilities are essential for maintaining and improving accessibility.

Conclusion

Web accessibility is a critical aspect of modern web development. It promotes inclusivity, legal compliance, and improved user experiences. By following the principles of perceivability, operability, understandability, and robustness, and by testing for accessibility, you can create web content that is welcoming and usable for all users, regardless of their abilities or disabilities. In the next section, we'll delve into building accessible web interfaces using HTML, CSS, and JavaScript.

Section 14.2: Building Accessible Web Interfaces

Building accessible web interfaces is a crucial aspect of web development. It ensures that people with disabilities can use and interact with your websites and web applications effectively. In this section, we'll explore best practices for creating accessible web interfaces using HTML, CSS, and JavaScript.

Semantic HTML

Semantic HTML refers to using HTML elements that convey meaning about the structure and content of a web page. It's the foundation of web accessibility because it allows assistive technologies to interpret and present content accurately. Here are some tips:

- Use proper headings (<h1>, <h2>, etc.) to structure your content hierarchically.

- Employ lists (<ul>, <ol>, <dl>) for structured data.

- Use semantic elements like <article>, <section>, <nav>, and <aside> to provide additional context.

- Include alternative text (alt attribute) for all images, ensuring that screen readers can describe them.

Keyboard Accessibility

Keyboard accessibility is essential for users who rely on keyboards or other input devices. Make sure your web interfaces can be navigated and interacted with using only the keyboard. Some tips:

- Ensure that all interactive elements (buttons, links, form fields) are keyboard focusable (tabindex attribute).

- Provide visible focus indicators (e.g., outlines) for keyboard focus to make it clear which element is currently active.

- Ensure that keyboard navigation follows a logical and intuitive order.

ARIA (Accessible Rich Internet Applications)

ARIA is a set of attributes that enhance the accessibility of dynamic content and widgets, such as menus, sliders, and modal dialogs. It helps screen readers and other assistive technologies understand and interact with web components. Some ARIA tips:

- Use ARIA roles and attributes when necessary to provide additional information to assistive technologies.

- Don't overuse ARIA; it should complement, not replace, semantic HTML.

- Test your ARIA implementation with screen readers to ensure compatibility.

CSS for Accessibility

CSS plays a role in accessibility as well. Some CSS tips:

- Ensure that text has sufficient contrast with its background to make it readable.

- Use responsive design techniques to ensure content is accessible on various screen sizes and devices.

- Be mindful of layout and avoid designs that rely heavily on absolute positioning, as this can disrupt the flow for screen reader users.

JavaScript and Accessibility

When adding interactivity with JavaScript, consider accessibility:

- Ensure that dynamic content updates are announced to screen reader users.

- Implement keyboard support for custom UI components, such as dropdowns or modals.

- Avoid focus traps, where users can't navigate away from an element.

Testing and User Feedback

Regularly test your web interfaces for accessibility using automated tools and manual testing with assistive technologies. Additionally, consider involving users with disabilities in usability testing to gather valuable feedback.

Conclusion

Building accessible web interfaces is not only a legal requirement in many jurisdictions but also a fundamental aspect of creating inclusive and user-friendly websites and web applications. By following these best practices and considering the needs of people with disabilities, you can make your web interfaces accessible to a broader audience. In the next section, we'll explore assistive technologies and testing methods for ensuring accessibility.

Section 14.3: Assistive Technologies and Testing

Assistive technologies (AT) are specialized software and hardware tools designed to assist people with disabilities in using computers and digital devices. They play a vital role in ensuring accessibility for individuals with different needs. In this section, we'll explore various types of assistive technologies and discuss how to test your web interfaces using them.

Types of Assistive Technologies

1. **Screen Readers**: Screen readers are software applications that convert digital text into synthesized speech or Braille

output. They allow users with visual impairments to navigate and interact with web content. Popular screen readers include JAWS, NVDA, and VoiceOver.

2. **Screen Magnifiers**: Screen magnifiers enlarge on-screen content, making it easier for users with low vision to read and interact with web pages. Users can control the level of magnification and pan around the screen to view different areas.

3. **Braille Displays**: Braille displays are tactile devices that present digital content in Braille characters. They provide a way for blind users to read and navigate text-based content.

4. **Speech Recognition Software**: Speech recognition software, like Dragon NaturallySpeaking, enables users with mobility impairments to control computers and dictate text using voice commands.

5. **Switch Access**: Switch access systems allow individuals with limited motor control to interact with computers and devices using switches or buttons they can control reliably. These switches can be activated by various body parts or specialized input devices.

6. **Keyboard Accessibility**: While not strictly assistive technology, keyboard navigation is crucial for many users with disabilities. Ensuring that your web interfaces are fully usable with a keyboard is a fundamental aspect of accessibility.

Testing with Assistive Technologies

To ensure your web interfaces are accessible, it's essential to test them with assistive technologies. Here's how you can get started:

1. **Screen Reader Testing**: Install and use popular screen readers like JAWS, NVDA, or VoiceOver. Navigate

through your website using keyboard shortcuts and listen to how the screen reader interprets and presents content. Pay attention to how it handles landmarks, headings, links, form controls, and ARIA attributes.

2. **Keyboard Testing**: Turn off the mouse and navigate your website using only the keyboard. Ensure that you can access all interactive elements and that focus indicators are visible and logical. Test keyboard accessibility in all parts of your web application, including forms and interactive widgets.

3. **Voice Recognition Testing**: If applicable, test voice recognition software to ensure that users can interact with your site using voice commands. Check if voice commands work as expected and that there are no conflicts with keyboard navigation.

4. **Braille Display Testing**: If you have access to a Braille display, test how your web content is presented in Braille. Ensure that it's structured correctly and that users can navigate and interact effectively.

5. **Switch Access Testing**: If your web application is intended for switch access users, test it with switch input devices. Ensure that users can navigate, activate controls, and perform essential tasks with switches.

6. **Accessibility APIs**: Familiarize yourself with the accessibility APIs (Application Programming Interfaces) provided by various operating systems and browsers. These APIs allow web developers to programmatically query and manipulate accessibility information. Test your web application's compatibility with these APIs to ensure assistive technologies can interact with it seamlessly.

Continuous Accessibility Testing

Accessibility is an ongoing process, and it's essential to include accessibility testing as part of your development and quality assurance workflow. Automated accessibility testing tools, such as Axe and Wave, can help identify common accessibility issues. However, manual testing with assistive technologies remains crucial for a comprehensive evaluation of accessibility.

By considering the needs of users with disabilities and testing your web interfaces with assistive technologies, you can create digital experiences that are inclusive and accessible to a broader audience. In the next section, we'll explore ARIA (Accessible Rich Internet Applications) and how it can enhance web accessibility.

Section 14.4: ARIA: Accessible Rich Internet Applications

ARIA (Accessible Rich Internet Applications) is a set of attributes that can be added to HTML elements to enhance the accessibility of dynamic web content and web applications. It was developed by the W3C (World Wide Web Consortium) to address the accessibility challenges posed by modern web technologies. In this section, we'll explore ARIA attributes and how they can be used to improve the accessibility of your web applications.

The Need for ARIA

Modern web applications often use complex and dynamic user interfaces that rely heavily on JavaScript and asynchronous updates. While these technologies provide a rich user experience, they can pose accessibility challenges, especially for users of assistive technologies such as screen readers. ARIA attributes were introduced to bridge this gap and make web applications more accessible.

ARIA Roles, States, and Properties

ARIA attributes fall into three main categories:

1. **Roles**: ARIA roles define the type of user interface element an HTML element represents. For example, you can use the role attribute to indicate that a div element functions as a button. This helps assistive technologies understand the purpose of the element.

```
<div role="button">Click me</div>
```

1. **States and Properties**: ARIA states and properties describe the current state or properties of an element. For example, you can use the aria-disabled attribute to indicate whether a button is disabled or not.

```
<button aria-disabled="true">Disabled Button</button>
```

How ARIA Benefits Accessibility

Here are some key ways in which ARIA can enhance accessibility:

1. **Semantic Clarity**: ARIA attributes provide semantic information about the purpose and behavior of UI elements. This helps screen readers and other assistive technologies convey the meaning of elements to users more accurately.
2. **Dynamic Content**: ARIA is particularly useful for dynamically updating content. It allows you to notify

assistive technologies when content changes occur, ensuring that users receive real-time information.

3. **Keyboard Navigation**: ARIA attributes can improve keyboard navigation by providing focus management and keyboard shortcuts for interactive elements, such as menus and modal dialogs.

4. **Form Accessibility**: ARIA can make form controls, such as sliders and date pickers, more accessible by providing additional information about their behavior and state changes.

5. **Widgets and Custom Components**: When creating custom widgets or components, ARIA allows you to define their roles and states, ensuring they are accessible to assistive technologies.

ARIA Best Practices

To effectively use ARIA for accessibility, consider the following best practices:

1. **Use Native Semantics**: Whenever possible, use native HTML elements and attributes with built-in accessibility features. Only use ARIA attributes when native HTML falls short.

2. **Provide Meaningful Labels**: Use the aria-label or aria-labelledby attribute to provide clear and concise labels for UI elements. Ensure that labels accurately convey the element's purpose.

3. **Update ARIA Attributes Dynamically**: If your web application updates content dynamically, be sure to update ARIA attributes accordingly to reflect the current state of the UI.

4. **Test with Assistive Technologies**: Regularly test your web

application with screen readers and other assistive technologies to ensure that ARIA attributes are correctly interpreted and provide an accessible user experience.

5. **Educate Your Team**: Ensure that your development team is familiar with ARIA and its best practices. Accessibility should be a collaborative effort.

By following ARIA best practices and integrating ARIA attributes into your web applications, you can make your digital content and interactions accessible to a wider audience, including individuals with disabilities. In the next section, we'll delve into the legal and ethical considerations surrounding web accessibility.

Section 14.5: Legal and Ethical Considerations

Ensuring web accessibility is not just a matter of goodwill; it's a legal and ethical responsibility. In this section, we'll explore the legal framework surrounding web accessibility and discuss the ethical reasons for prioritizing accessibility in web development.

Legal Framework

1. Americans with Disabilities Act (ADA): The ADA is a U.S. federal law that prohibits discrimination against people with disabilities. It covers both physical and digital spaces, which means that websites and web applications must be accessible to individuals with disabilities. Courts have increasingly interpreted the ADA to apply to the web.

2. Section 508: Section 508 of the Rehabilitation Act requires federal agencies in the United States to make their electronic and information technology accessible to people with disabilities. This includes websites and digital documents.

3. Web Content Accessibility Guidelines (WCAG): While not a law itself, WCAG is a widely accepted set of guidelines for web accessibility. Many countries, including Canada and the European Union, have adopted WCAG as the standard for web accessibility compliance. Following WCAG guidelines can help organizations meet legal requirements.

4. European Accessibility Act (EAA): The EAA, which came into effect in 2021, mandates that key digital services and products in the European Union must be accessible. This includes websites, mobile apps, and digital documents.

5. Accessibility Lawsuits: In recent years, there has been a significant increase in web accessibility-related lawsuits. Organizations that do not prioritize accessibility risk legal action, which can result in substantial legal fees and damages.

Ethical Considerations

1. Inclusivity: Web accessibility is about making the digital world inclusive for all. By prioritizing accessibility, you are taking a stance for inclusivity and equal opportunities. It aligns with the ethical principle of treating all individuals with respect and dignity.

2. Social Responsibility: In a digitally connected world, your web content and services play a significant role in people's lives. Prioritizing accessibility is a demonstration of social responsibility, acknowledging the importance of making digital resources accessible to everyone.

3. Customer Experience: Accessibility improvements often enhance the overall user experience. When you prioritize accessibility, you not only serve individuals with disabilities but also create a better experience for all users, potentially leading to increased customer satisfaction.

4. Brand Reputation: Organizations that are committed to accessibility tend to have a better brand reputation. Conversely, negative publicity related to accessibility issues can harm a brand's image and credibility.

5. Innovation: Embracing accessibility can drive innovation. Many accessibility features, such as voice commands and screen readers, have led to innovative technologies that benefit a broader audience.

6. Global Reach: Prioritizing accessibility ensures that your digital content can be accessed by a global audience. This can open up new markets and opportunities for your organization.

Conclusion

Web accessibility is not merely a checkbox but a moral and legal imperative. It's a commitment to making the internet a more inclusive and equitable space. By following legal requirements, such as the ADA and WCAG, and embracing accessibility as an ethical principle, you contribute to a digital world that values diversity and ensures that no one is left behind. In the final chapters of this book, we'll explore advanced topics in JavaScript and the future of web development, emphasizing the importance of continued learning and adaptation in this ever-evolving field.

Chapter 15: Internationalization and Localization

Section 15.1: The Importance of Internationalization

Internationalization, often abbreviated as i18n (because there are 18 letters between 'i' and 'n' in the word), is a crucial aspect of modern web development. It refers to the process of designing and adapting your software or website to be usable in different languages and regions. Localization, abbreviated as l10n, is a subset of internationalization and involves translating your application's content and adapting it to specific cultural and linguistic contexts.

Why Internationalization Matters

1. **Global Reach**: With the internet connecting people worldwide, your website or application can potentially reach users from diverse backgrounds and languages. Internationalization ensures that your product is accessible to a broader audience.

2. **Market Expansion**: Expanding your business to international markets can significantly increase your customer base and revenue. However, to succeed, you need to offer content in the local language and cater to regional preferences.

3. **Legal and Compliance**: Some regions have specific legal requirements regarding language and accessibility. Internationalization helps you stay compliant with these regulations.

4. **Enhanced User Experience**: When users can interact with your application in their native language, it enhances their

overall experience and increases user satisfaction.

5. **Competitive Advantage**: Being able to offer your product in multiple languages and regions can give you a competitive edge over others who only cater to a single market.

6. **Cultural Sensitivity**: Different cultures have distinct norms, values, and sensitivities. Internationalization allows you to adapt your content and user interface to respect these cultural differences.

Key Components of Internationalization

To implement internationalization effectively, consider the following key components:

- **Content Translation**: Translate all textual content into multiple languages. This includes user interface elements, labels, error messages, and user-generated content.

- **Date and Time Formatting**: Adapt date and time formats to match regional preferences. Different countries use different date formats (e.g., MM/DD/YYYY or DD/MM/YYYY), and time formats (e.g., 12-hour or 24-hour clock).

- **Number and Currency Formatting**: Display numbers and currencies in the format preferred by each region. This includes decimal separators, thousand separators, and currency symbols.

- **Character Encoding**: Ensure your application can handle characters from various languages and writing systems. Use Unicode (UTF-8) encoding to support a wide range of characters.

• **Locale Detection**: Detect users' preferred language and region based on their browser settings or user preferences. This allows your application to automatically switch to the appropriate language and format.

• **Content Expansion**: Consider that translated content might be longer or shorter than the original. Ensure your layout can accommodate these variations without breaking.

• **Cultural Adaptation**: Be aware of cultural differences in images, icons, colors, and symbols. What is considered acceptable or offensive can vary between cultures.

• **Testing and Quality Assurance**: Rigorously test your internationalized application with users from different regions to identify and fix any issues related to language, date/time formats, or cultural sensitivities.

Internationalization is not a one-time effort but an ongoing process that evolves with your application and its user base. Properly internationalized applications are more inclusive, accessible, and user-friendly, making them more likely to succeed in a globalized world.

Section 15.2: JavaScript Internationalization API (Intl)

The JavaScript Internationalization API, commonly referred to as Intl, is a built-in JavaScript feature introduced in ECMAScript Internationalization API Specification (ECMA-402) that provides developers with powerful tools for handling internationalization and localization in web applications. It allows you to format dates, times, numbers, and currencies according to different locales and languages.

Key Intl Objects

The Intl API includes several objects for different internationalization tasks:

1. **Intl.DateTimeFormat**: This object is used for formatting dates and times according to the specified locale. You can customize date and time formatting, including options like date style, time style, time zone, and more.

```
const date = new Date();

const locale = 'en-US';

const options = { year: 'numeric', month: 'long', day: 'numeric' };

const formattedDate = new Intl.DateTimeFormat(locale, options).format(date);

console.log(formattedDate); // Output: "October 31, 2023"
```

1. **Intl.NumberFormat**: This object helps you format numbers, including decimals, percentages, and currencies, based on the specified locale. You can control the number of decimal places, use group separators, and format currencies with the correct symbols.

```
const number = 1234567.89;
```

```
const locale = 'de-DE';

const options = { style: 'currency', currency: 'EUR' };

const formattedNumber = new Intl.NumberFormat(locale, options).format(number);

console.log(formattedNumber); // Output: "1.234.567,89 €"
```

1. **Intl.Collator**: This object helps you perform string comparison and sorting operations based on the specified locale. It considers language-specific rules for character comparison, which is crucial for proper sorting in different languages.

```
const collator = new Intl.Collator('es-ES');

const words = ['manzana', 'árbol', 'Zorro', 'uña'];

const sortedWords = words.sort(collator.compare);

console.log(sortedWords); // Output: ["árbol", "manzana", "uña", "Zorro"]
```

1. **Intl.ListFormat**: This object allows you to format lists of items, such as arrays, according to the conventions of the specified locale. It handles conjunctions, disjunctions, and unit separators as per language-specific rules.

```
const items = ['apple', 'banana', 'cherry'];

const locale = 'fr-FR';
```

```javascript
const listFormatter = new Intl.ListFormat(locale, { style:
'long', type: 'conjunction' });

const formattedList = listFormatter.format(items);

console.log(formattedList); // Output: "pomme, banane et
cerise"
```

1. **Intl.RelativeTimeFormat**: This object provides a way to
   format relative time units (e.g., "in 5 minutes" or "3 days
   ago") according to the specified locale. It's especially useful
   for displaying dynamic time-related information.

```javascript
const timeInSeconds = 300;

const locale = 'ja-JP';

const formatter = new Intl.RelativeTimeFormat(locale, {
numeric: 'auto' });

const                    formattedTime                    =
formatter.format(-timeInSeconds, 'second');

console.log(formattedTime); // Output: "5◇◇"
```

Browser Compatibility

The Intl API is widely supported in modern browsers, making it
a robust choice for internationalization tasks in web applications.
However, ensure that your target audience uses browsers that
support Intl or consider using a polyfill for older browsers if
necessary.

By leveraging the JavaScript Internationalization API, you can
efficiently handle internationalization and localization requirements

in your web applications, providing a more inclusive and user-friendly experience for a global audience.

Section 15.3: Language and Region Detection

Language and region detection is a crucial part of internationalization and localization in web applications. It involves identifying the user's preferred language and region settings to provide content that matches their preferences. The JavaScript Internationalization API (Intl) provides features to help detect and work with these settings.

Navigator Language

The navigator.language property is a simple way to access the user's preferred language. It returns a string representing the language tag, which typically consists of a language code and optionally a region or country code.

const userLanguage = navigator.language;

console.log(userLanguage); // *Example output: "en-US"*

By default, navigator.language provides the language and region based on the user's browser settings. Developers can use this information to dynamically adjust the content of their web applications.

Intl.getCanonicalLocales()

The Intl.getCanonicalLocales() method allows you to normalize and validate language and region codes. This is important for ensuring that your application handles language tags correctly and consistently.

```
const locales = ['en-us', 'fr-fr', 'ja-JP', 'de'];
```

```
const canonicalLocales = locales.map((locale) =>
Intl.getCanonicalLocales(locale));
```

```
console.log(canonicalLocales);
```

```
// Example output: ["en-US", "fr-FR", "ja-JP", "de"]
```

This method takes an array of language tags and returns an array of canonicalized and validated locales.

Language and Region Matching

To provide content tailored to the user's language and region, you can use the Intl.Locale object to perform matching between available locales and the user's preferences. This allows you to select the most suitable locale for presenting content.

```
const userLocale = new Intl.Locale(navigator.language);
```

```
const availableLocales = ['en-US', 'fr-FR', 'es-ES', 'de-DE'];
```

```
const matchedLocale = Intl.Locale
```

```
.supportedLocalesOf(availableLocales, { localeMatcher: 'lookup'
})[0];
```

```
console.log(matchedLocale.toString()); // Example output based on
user locale
```

In this example, Intl.Locale.supportedLocalesOf() is used to find the best match between the user's locale and the available locales, based on the "lookup" locale matcher. The matched locale can then be used to present content that aligns with the user's preferences.

Language and Region Switching

Web applications often provide users with the ability to switch languages or regions dynamically. To achieve this, you can store and manage user preferences, and then use the Intl API to update the displayed content accordingly.

const userPreferences = {

language: 'fr-FR',

region: 'CA',

};

const userLocale = **new** Intl.Locale(userPreferences.language, { region: userPreferences.region });

// Use userLocale for content rendering

By storing and updating user preferences and creating an Intl.Locale object based on those preferences, you can maintain a customized experience for users who want to switch languages or regions while using your web application.

Browser Compatibility

The navigator.language property is well-supported across modern browsers. However, it's essential to test your application in different browsers to ensure consistent behavior.

Overall, language and region detection is a fundamental aspect of creating a user-friendly and globally accessible web application. Leveraging the JavaScript Internationalization API can greatly simplify the process of working with language and region preferences.

Section 15.4: Localization Techniques

Localization involves adapting your web application's content to different languages, regions, and cultures. It goes beyond language translation and encompasses various aspects, including formatting dates, numbers, and currencies, as well as adjusting layouts and images for different cultures. In this section, we'll explore techniques and tools for achieving effective localization in your JavaScript applications.

Using Intl for Formatting

The Intl object in JavaScript provides powerful tools for formatting and parsing data according to the user's locale. It includes methods like Intl.DateTimeFormat for formatting dates and times, Intl.NumberFormat for formatting numbers, and Intl.Collator for string comparison based on sorting rules of the user's locale.

Here's an example of formatting a date using Intl.DateTimeFormat:

```javascript
const date = new Date();

const userLocale = 'fr-FR';

const formattedDate = new Intl.DateTimeFormat(userLocale).format(date);

console.log(formattedDate); // Example output: "05/11/2023" (for French locale)
```

By creating an Intl object with the user's locale, you can ensure that dates, numbers, and strings are displayed in a culturally appropriate manner.

String Resource Bundles

Localization often involves managing large sets of translated text strings. To handle this efficiently, you can use string resource bundles. These are JSON or JavaScript files that map keys to translated values for different languages.

```javascript
// Example string resource bundle for English and French

const resources = {

en: {

greeting: 'Hello, World!',

welcome: 'Welcome to our website.',

},

fr: {

greeting: 'Bonjour, le Monde !',

welcome: 'Bienvenue sur notre site Web.',

},

};

// Accessing localized strings based on user's language

const userLocale = 'fr';

const localizedStrings = resources[userLocale];

console.log(localizedStrings.greeting); // Example output: "Bonjour, le Monde !"
```

By organizing strings in resource bundles, you can easily switch between languages based on the user's preference without cluttering your codebase.

Reacting to Language Changes

When users switch languages, your application should dynamically update its content. In a JavaScript framework like React, you can achieve this by using state management and context to propagate the selected language throughout your components.

Here's a simplified example using React and the Context API:

```
// LanguageContext.js

import React, { createContext, useContext, useState } from 'react';

const LanguageContext = createContext();

export function LanguageProvider({ children }) {

const [language, setLanguage] = useState('en');

return (

<LanguageContext.Provider value={{ language, setLanguage }}>

{children}

</LanguageContext.Provider>

);

}

export function useLanguage() {

return useContext(LanguageContext);
```

```
}
```

With this setup, you can wrap your application with the LanguageProvider and use the useLanguage hook in components to access and set the language. When the user changes the language, components subscribed to the context will re-render with the updated content.

Tools and Libraries

For larger applications, consider using popular JavaScript libraries like i18next or react-i18next to simplify the localization process. These libraries offer features like string interpolation, pluralization, and date formatting, making it easier to manage translations and dynamically update content.

In conclusion, effective localization is essential for making your web application accessible and user-friendly to a global audience. Leveraging JavaScript's Intl object, organizing string resources, and using context-based language switching are key techniques to ensure a seamless localization experience for your users.

Section 15.5: Challenges and Best Practices

Localization and internationalization (l10n and i18n) are essential for reaching a global audience, but they come with challenges and best practices that every developer should be aware of.

Challenges in Localization

1. String Expansion and Contraction

Languages have different sentence structures, which can lead to the expansion or contraction of text. For example, a sentence in English may be shorter or longer when translated into another language. This can affect the layout and design of your user interface.

2. Pluralization and Gender Neutrality

Some languages have complex rules for pluralization, and gender-specific words may require different translations. Handling these variations programmatically can be challenging.

3. Date and Time Formats

Different cultures have unique date and time formatting conventions. Ensuring that your application correctly formats dates and times according to the user's locale is crucial.

4. Right-to-Left (RTL) Languages

Languages like Arabic and Hebrew are written from right to left. Adapting your UI to support RTL layouts can be complex, requiring careful consideration of text direction and layout adjustments.

5. Cultural Sensitivity

Cultural norms and taboos can vary widely. Ensure that your content is culturally sensitive and appropriate for all audiences.

Best Practices in Localization

1. Plan Early

Consider localization from the beginning of your project. Internationalization should be part of the design and architecture, not a feature added as an afterthought.

2. Use String Resource Bundles

Store all translatable strings in resource bundles, and avoid hardcoding text throughout your codebase. This makes it easier to manage translations and switch between languages.

3. Externalize Text

Externalizing text means separating it from code. Avoid embedding text directly in your JavaScript files or HTML templates. Instead, load translations dynamically from resource bundles.

4. Choose the Right Tools

Use localization and internationalization libraries and frameworks that fit your project's needs. Libraries like i18next, react-i18next, or Format.js can streamline the process.

5. Test Extensively

Thoroughly test your application with different languages and locales. Pay attention to string expansion, layout issues, and the correct rendering of special characters.

6. Maintain Consistency

Maintain consistent terminology and phrasing across your application. Inconsistent translations can confuse users.

7. Provide Context

Help translators by providing context for text strings. Clear context ensures accurate translations.

8. Document Guidelines

Document guidelines for translators, including instructions for handling placeholders, formatting, and plurals. Clear guidelines lead to better translations.

9. Consider Accessibility

Ensure that your localized content remains accessible. Screen readers and assistive technologies should work seamlessly with translated text.

10. Stay Informed

Stay updated on localization best practices and changes in the languages you support. Languages evolve, and your application should keep up.

In summary, while localization and internationalization present challenges, following best practices can help you provide a seamless experience for users worldwide. Plan ahead, use the right tools, and test rigorously to ensure that your application is truly global-ready.

Chapter 16: Advanced Topics in JavaScript

In this chapter, we delve into advanced topics in JavaScript, exploring areas that extend beyond the typical web development landscape. These advanced topics are at the forefront of JavaScript's capabilities, pushing the boundaries of what you can achieve with this versatile language.

Section 16.1: Web Components and Custom Elements

Web Components are a set of web platform APIs that allow you to create new custom, reusable, encapsulated HTML tags to use in web pages and web apps. They enable developers to define their own HTML elements with custom behavior and styling, encapsulating them from the rest of the page and other components. This section explores the concept of Web Components and Custom Elements in JavaScript.

Understanding Web Components

Web Components consist of three main technologies:

1. **Custom Elements:** Custom Elements allow you to define your own HTML elements with a custom name and behavior. For example, you can create a <my-button> element with specific functionality.
2. **Shadow DOM:** The Shadow DOM provides encapsulation by creating a separate, isolated DOM tree for each custom element. This prevents CSS and JavaScript conflicts with the rest of the page.

3. **HTML Templates:** HTML Templates allow you to define reusable chunks of DOM that can be cloned and inserted into the Shadow DOM or the main document.

Creating a Custom Element

To create a Custom Element, you'll need to use the CustomElementRegistry.define() method. Here's a simplified example of creating a custom element called <my-greeting>:

```javascript
class MyGreeting extends HTMLElement {

constructor() {

super();
// Create a Shadow DOM for this element

const shadow = this.attachShadow({ mode: 'open' });
// Create a paragraph element and add it to the Shadow DOM

const p = document.createElement('p');

p.textContent = 'Hello, Web Component!';

shadow.appendChild(p);

}

}
// Define the custom element

customElements.define('my-greeting', MyGreeting);
```

Using a Custom Element

Once defined, you can use your custom element in your HTML like any other HTML element:

<my-greeting></my-greeting>

Benefits of Web Components

Web Components offer several advantages:

- **Reusability:** You can use your custom elements across different projects.

- **Isolation:** Shadow DOM prevents styles and scripts from leaking out or interfering with your component.

- **Encapsulation:** Web Components allow you to encapsulate complex functionality in a single element.

Browser Support

While Web Components are a powerful technology, browser support may vary, and polyfills are often required to ensure compatibility with older browsers.

In this section, we've explored the basics of Web Components and Custom Elements. They provide a way to create encapsulated, reusable components, making your web development projects more modular and maintainable. As the web ecosystem continues to evolve, understanding these advanced topics becomes increasingly valuable.

Section 16.2: Serverless Computing with AWS Lambda

Serverless computing is a cloud computing model that allows developers to build and run applications without managing servers. AWS Lambda, offered by Amazon Web Services (AWS), is a leading platform for implementing serverless functions and applications. In this section, we'll explore the concept of serverless computing and delve into using AWS Lambda with JavaScript.

What Is Serverless Computing?

Serverless computing, often referred to as Function as a Service (FaaS), abstracts the underlying infrastructure and server management away from developers. Instead of provisioning and managing servers, developers focus on writing code in the form of small, stateless functions. These functions are executed in response to events or triggers, such as HTTP requests, database changes, or file uploads.

AWS Lambda Basics

AWS Lambda is a serverless computing service provided by AWS. It allows you to run code in response to various AWS events or HTTP requests without the need to provision or manage servers. Here are some key concepts related to AWS Lambda:

- **Lambda Function:** A Lambda function is a piece of code that runs in response to an event. You can write Lambda functions in various programming languages, including JavaScript (Node.js).

- **Event Sources:** Lambda functions can be triggered by various event sources, such as AWS S3 bucket changes,

AWS API Gateway requests, or AWS CloudWatch Events.

- **Execution Environment:** AWS Lambda manages the execution environment for your functions, including provisioning and scaling resources as needed.

Creating a Simple AWS Lambda Function

Let's create a simple Lambda function in JavaScript to get a feel for how it works. Suppose you want to create a function that calculates the square of a number.

```javascript
exports.handler = async (event) => {

const number = event.number || 0;

const square = number * number;

return {

statusCode: 200,

body: JSON.stringify({ result: square }),

};

};
```

In this example, we export a function named handler that receives an event object. It calculates the square of a number provided in the event and returns the result in JSON format.

Triggering Lambda Functions

Lambda functions can be triggered in various ways, such as through an HTTP request or an AWS service event. To trigger a Lambda function via HTTP, you can use AWS API Gateway to create an API and connect it to your Lambda function. This enables you to build serverless web applications with endpoints powered by Lambda functions.

Benefits of Serverless Computing

Serverless computing offers several advantages:

- **Cost-Efficiency:** You only pay for the actual compute time used by your functions, making it cost-effective for applications with varying workloads.

- **Scalability:** Serverless platforms automatically scale your functions in response to incoming traffic, ensuring high availability and performance.

- **Simplified Operations:** You don't need to worry about server maintenance, operating system updates, or infrastructure provisioning.

Considerations and Challenges

While serverless computing offers many benefits, it's essential to consider potential challenges, such as cold starts (initial function invocation latency), resource limits, and vendor lock-in. Additionally, monitoring and debugging in a serverless environment may require different tools and approaches.

In summary, serverless computing with AWS Lambda simplifies application development by abstracting server management and enabling developers to focus on writing code. It's a powerful approach for building scalable and cost-efficient applications, especially when combined with the flexibility of JavaScript for defining Lambda functions.

Section 16.3: WebAssembly and JavaScript

WebAssembly, often abbreviated as wasm, is an emerging technology that allows running low-level code directly in web browsers. While JavaScript has been the primary language for web development, WebAssembly introduces a new way to execute code with near-native performance. In this section, we'll explore the relationship between WebAssembly and JavaScript, and how they can be used together to enhance web applications.

Understanding WebAssembly

WebAssembly is a binary instruction format that is designed to be a portable target for the compilation of high-level programming languages like C, C++, and Rust. It provides a virtual machine that can execute code at near-native speed in web browsers. WebAssembly aims to improve web application performance and open up the web platform to a wider range of programming languages.

WebAssembly Modules

WebAssembly code is typically bundled into modules, which are binary files that contain low-level instructions. These modules can be loaded and executed by web browsers. JavaScript plays a crucial role in interacting with and controlling WebAssembly modules.

Interoperability with JavaScript

While WebAssembly can run code independently, it often needs to communicate with JavaScript to interact with the web page, access the Document Object Model (DOM), handle user interactions, and more. JavaScript and WebAssembly can work together seamlessly, allowing developers to combine the performance benefits of WebAssembly with the flexibility and functionality of JavaScript.

Here's an example of how you can use JavaScript to load and interact with a WebAssembly module:

```
// Load a WebAssembly module

fetch('module.wasm')

.then(response => response.arrayBuffer())

.then(bytes => WebAssembly.instantiate(bytes))

.then(result => {

const instance = result.instance;

// Call a WebAssembly function from JavaScript

const result = instance.exports.myFunction(42);

console.log('Result from WebAssembly:', result);

})

.catch(error => console.error('Error loading WebAssembly module:', error));
```

In this code snippet:

1. We use the fetch API to load a WebAssembly binary file (module.wasm).
2. Once the binary data is loaded, we use WebAssembly.instantiate to compile and instantiate the

module.

3. We can then access functions and data from the WebAssembly module using instance.exports.
4. Finally, we call a WebAssembly function (myFunction) and log the result in the JavaScript console.

Use Cases for WebAssembly and JavaScript

WebAssembly is particularly useful for tasks that require high performance, such as gaming, video editing, and scientific simulations. It allows developers to port existing C/C++ codebases to the web, taking advantage of the web platform's reach while maintaining performance.

However, JavaScript remains essential for web development, especially for building user interfaces, handling user interactions, and managing web page content. WebAssembly and JavaScript can complement each other to create powerful and efficient web applications.

Future of WebAssembly and JavaScript

The adoption of WebAssembly continues to grow, and it's expected to play a more prominent role in web development. In the future, we can anticipate better tooling, improved integration between WebAssembly and JavaScript, and broader support across browsers and platforms. Developers should consider how to leverage both technologies to create modern web applications that deliver optimal performance and user experiences.

Section 16.4: Machine Learning in JavaScript

Machine learning (ML) has become an integral part of various applications and services, and JavaScript developers can leverage ML in web development through various libraries and frameworks. In this section, we'll explore the possibilities of incorporating machine learning into JavaScript projects and some of the tools available for doing so.

The Rise of ML in JavaScript

Machine learning has traditionally been associated with languages like Python and libraries like TensorFlow and PyTorch. However, with the advancement of web technologies, JavaScript has also become a viable option for implementing and deploying machine learning models in web applications. This shift is driven by the need for real-time and client-side ML capabilities.

JavaScript ML Libraries

Several JavaScript libraries and frameworks provide tools for machine learning and neural networks. Here are a few notable ones:

TensorFlow.js

TensorFlow.js is a JavaScript library developed by Google that brings the capabilities of TensorFlow to the web browser and Node.js. It allows developers to build and train machine learning models using JavaScript and deploy them directly in web applications.

```javascript
// Example of using TensorFlow.js for image classification

const tf = require('@tensorflow/tfjs-node');

const mobilenet = require('@tensorflow-models/mobilenet');

async function classifyImage(imageElement) {

const model = await mobilenet.load();
```

```javascript
const predictions = await model.classify(imageElement);

return predictions;

}
```

Brain.js

Brain.js is a neural network library for JavaScript that simplifies the process of creating and training neural networks. It's particularly well-suited for tasks like classification, regression, and time series forecasting.

```javascript
// Example of using Brain.js for XOR problem

const brain = require('brain.js');

const net = new brain.NeuralNetwork();

net.train([{ input: [0, 0], output: [0] }, { input: [1, 0], output: [1] }, { input: [0, 1], output: [1] }, { input: [1, 1], output: [0] }]);

const output = net.run([1, 0]);

console.log(output); // Output: [0.987]
```

ml5.js

ml5.js is a friendly machine learning library built on top of TensorFlow.js. It simplifies the integration of machine learning models and provides pre-trained models for various tasks like image classification and pose estimation.

```javascript
// Example of using ml5.js for image classification

const ml5 = require('ml5');
```

```javascript
const imageClassifier = ml5.imageClassifier('MobileNet', () => {

console.log('Model loaded');

});

const img = document.getElementById('image');

imageClassifier.classify(img, (error, results) => {

if (!error) {

console.log(results);

}

});
```

Use Cases for JavaScript ML

Integrating machine learning into JavaScript applications opens up a wide range of possibilities. Some common use cases include:

- **Image and Video Recognition:** ML models can classify objects, detect faces, and recognize gestures in real-time.

- **Natural Language Processing (NLP):** JavaScript can be used to analyze and process text data, perform sentiment analysis, and build chatbots.

- **Recommendation Systems:** ML can power recommendation engines that suggest products, content, or services to users based on their behavior.

- **Anomaly Detection:** ML models can detect anomalies in data, helping to identify unusual patterns or outliers.

Challenges and Considerations

While JavaScript-based machine learning has many advantages, it also comes with challenges:

- **Performance:** ML computations can be resource-intensive, and client-side ML may not be suitable for all devices and browsers.

- **Model Size:** ML models can be large, leading to longer loading times for web applications.

- **Privacy and Security:** Handling user data for ML tasks requires careful consideration of privacy and security concerns.

Developers interested in incorporating machine learning into JavaScript projects should assess the specific requirements of their applications and choose the appropriate libraries and tools accordingly. With the right approach, JavaScript can become a powerful platform for implementing ML solutions on the web.

Section 16.5: Blockchain and Cryptocurrency Integration

Blockchain technology and cryptocurrencies have gained significant attention in recent years. While they are typically associated with languages like Python and Solidity, JavaScript can also be used to interact with blockchain networks and integrate cryptocurrencies into web applications. In this section, we'll explore the possibilities of using JavaScript for blockchain and cryptocurrency integration.

Blockchain Basics

Blockchain is a decentralized and distributed ledger technology that records transactions across a network of computers. It is most commonly known for its use in cryptocurrencies like Bitcoin and Ethereum, but its applications extend beyond digital currencies. Blockchain offers transparency, security, and immutability, making it suitable for various use cases, including supply chain management, voting systems, and more.

JavaScript and Blockchain

JavaScript developers can interact with blockchain networks and smart contracts through web3 libraries like Web3.js and ethers.js. These libraries provide APIs for connecting to blockchain networks, sending transactions, and reading data from smart contracts. Here's an example of using Web3.js to interact with Ethereum:

```javascript
// Example of using Web3.js to interact with Ethereum

const Web3 = require('web3');

const web3 = new Web3('https://mainnet.infura.io/v3/YOUR_INFURA_PROJECT_ID');

web3.eth.getBlockNumber()

.then(blockNumber => {

console.log('Latest block number:', blockNumber);

})

.catch(error => {

console.error('Error:', error);
```

```
});
```

Cryptocurrency Wallets

JavaScript can also be used to create cryptocurrency wallets and manage digital assets within web applications. Wallet libraries like ethers.js and web3.js provide functionalities to generate wallets, sign transactions, and check account balances. Developers can build user-friendly interfaces for cryptocurrency management using these libraries.

Use Cases for Blockchain and Cryptocurrency Integration

Integrating blockchain and cryptocurrencies into web applications can enable various use cases:

- **Payment Systems:** Accepting cryptocurrency payments for products or services, providing a secure and borderless payment option.

- **Tokenization:** Creating and managing custom tokens on blockchain networks for crowdfunding, loyalty programs, or in-app purchases.

- **Decentralized Applications (DApps):** Building decentralized applications that interact with smart contracts to perform actions without relying on central authorities.

- **Supply Chain:** Using blockchain to track and verify the origin and authenticity of products in a supply chain.

- **Identity Verification:** Implementing blockchain-based identity verification and authentication systems for enhanced security and privacy.

Challenges and Considerations

While blockchain and cryptocurrencies offer exciting opportunities, there are challenges and considerations when integrating them with JavaScript web applications:

- **Complexity:** Blockchain development can be complex, and developers need to understand how blockchain networks and smart contracts work.

- **Security:** Ensuring the security of cryptocurrency wallets and handling private keys securely is crucial to prevent theft or loss of digital assets.

- **Regulatory Compliance:** Staying compliant with relevant regulations and tax laws when dealing with cryptocurrencies is essential.

- **Scalability:** Blockchain networks may have limitations in terms of scalability and transaction speed, which can impact the user experience.

Developers interested in blockchain and cryptocurrency integration should thoroughly research the specific blockchain platform they plan to work with, understand the associated risks, and consider the legal and regulatory aspects of their projects. With the right knowledge and precautions, JavaScript can be a valuable tool for building blockchain-powered applications and services.

Chapter 17: Building a Real-World Project

Section 17.1: Project Planning and Architecture

In this section, we'll delve into the crucial aspects of planning and architecting a real-world JavaScript project. Building a substantial project requires careful thought, organization, and a clear vision from the start.

Project Planning

Define Your Goals and Objectives

Before writing a single line of code, it's essential to define the project's goals and objectives. What problem are you trying to solve? Who is the target audience? What are the key features and functionalities the project should have? Clear objectives provide direction and help prioritize tasks.

Create a Project Scope

Determine the scope of your project. What should be included and what should be left out? Create a list of features, modules, and components required for the project. This step helps manage expectations and prevents feature creep.

Plan Your Timeline

Set realistic deadlines and milestones for your project. Consider dependencies between tasks and allocate sufficient time for testing and debugging. A well-planned timeline helps in project management and ensures that you stay on track.

Identify Risks

Identify potential risks and challenges that may arise during the project. It's essential to have contingency plans in place to address these issues promptly. Common risks include technical difficulties, resource constraints, and changes in requirements.

Project Architecture

Choose the Right Architecture

Selecting an appropriate architecture is crucial for project success. Depending on the project's size and complexity, you might opt for a monolithic architecture, microservices, or a serverless architecture. The choice will impact scalability, maintainability, and deployment options.

Design the Data Model

Create a data model that defines how data will be structured and stored. Choose a database system that suits your project's requirements, whether it's a relational database, NoSQL database, or a combination of both.

Define the Tech Stack

Select the technologies, libraries, and frameworks that align with your project's goals. Consider factors like performance, community support, and your team's familiarity with the chosen tools.

Plan for Scalability

Think about how the project will scale as it grows. Implementing scalability from the beginning can save you from major re-architecting efforts down the road. This may involve using load balancers, caching, or serverless solutions.

Security Considerations

Security should be a top priority. Plan for authentication, authorization, data encryption, and protection against common web vulnerabilities such as cross-site scripting (XSS) and SQL injection.

Documentation and Communication

Document Your Code

Maintaining clear and up-to-date documentation is essential for team collaboration and project sustainability. Document code, APIs, and configurations comprehensively.

Communication Plan

Establish effective communication channels within your team. Regular meetings, issue tracking, and collaboration tools like Slack or Microsoft Teams can streamline communication.

Conclusion

Proper project planning and architecture are the foundation of a successful JavaScript project. By defining your objectives, scoping your project, and making informed decisions about architecture and technology stack, you set your project on the path to success. In the following sections, we'll explore frontend and backend development, integration and testing, deployment, and maintenance to complete the picture of building a real-world project.

Section 17.2: Frontend Development

Frontend development is a critical aspect of building a real-world project. It's responsible for creating the user interface and ensuring a seamless user experience. In this section, we'll explore key considerations and best practices for frontend development.

User Interface (UI) Design

The UI design phase involves creating a visual representation of your project's interface. Designers work on layout, color schemes, typography, and interactive elements to make the application visually appealing and user-friendly. Collaboration between designers and developers is essential to ensure the design can be effectively implemented.

Responsive Design

With the variety of devices and screen sizes available today, it's crucial to make your project responsive. Responsive design ensures that your application looks and works well on desktops, laptops, tablets, and smartphones. CSS frameworks like Bootstrap and Flexbox can simplify responsive design implementation.

Component-Based Development

Component-based development promotes code reusability and maintainability. Break your UI into smaller, reusable components. JavaScript frameworks like React, Vue.js, and Angular are well-suited for building applications using this approach. Each component focuses on a specific part of the UI and can be easily reused across the project.

State Management

As your project grows in complexity, managing the application's state becomes more challenging. State management libraries like Redux (for React) and Vuex (for Vue.js) help centralize and manage the application's state. They provide predictable ways to handle data changes and interactions across components.

Performance Optimization

Optimizing frontend performance is crucial for delivering a fast and responsive user experience. Techniques like code splitting, lazy loading, and minimizing HTTP requests can significantly improve loading times. Tools like Google's Lighthouse can help identify performance bottlenecks.

Frontend Testing

Testing is an integral part of frontend development. Automated testing tools like Jest, Mocha, and Cypress can be used to write unit tests, integration tests, and end-to-end tests. Writing tests ensures that your frontend code works as expected and helps catch regressions early.

Accessibility

Accessibility is about making your project usable by people with disabilities. Following accessibility best practices ensures that your application can be navigated and used by individuals with various impairments. Tools like screen readers, keyboard navigation, and semantic HTML elements play a crucial role in accessibility.

Cross-Browser Compatibility

Web applications should work consistently across different web browsers. Testing your project in major browsers like Chrome, Firefox, Safari, and Edge is essential. CSS prefixes and feature detection can help handle browser-specific issues.

Internationalization (i18n) and Localization (l10n)

If your project targets a global audience, consider internationalization and localization. Internationalization involves making your application adaptable to different languages and regions. Localization involves translating and adapting the content for specific locales. JavaScript's Internationalization API (Intl) can assist in these efforts.

Progressive Web App (PWA)

Consider turning your project into a Progressive Web App (PWA). PWAs provide a native app-like experience on the web, including offline access, push notifications, and a home screen icon. Service workers and web app manifests are key components of PWAs.

In conclusion, frontend development is a multifaceted discipline that requires attention to design, performance, accessibility, and internationalization. Choosing the right technology stack, following best practices, and collaborating effectively with backend developers and designers are essential for a successful frontend development process. In the next section, we'll explore backend development, which is equally critical in building a real-world project.

Section 17.3: Backend Development

Backend development is the foundation of a real-world project, responsible for server-side logic, data management, and communication with the frontend. In this section, we'll delve into the key aspects of backend development.

Technology Stack

Selecting the right technology stack is crucial for backend development. Popular backend languages include Node.js, Python, Ruby, PHP, and Java. The choice depends on project requirements, scalability, and developer expertise. Node.js, with its non-blocking event-driven architecture, is a popular choice for building scalable web applications.

Server Setup

Setting up a server environment involves choosing a hosting provider, configuring server instances, and managing server security. Cloud providers like AWS, Azure, Google Cloud, and Heroku offer scalable and reliable server hosting options. Proper server configuration, including firewall settings and security updates, is essential to safeguard your application.

API Design

Backend development often involves creating APIs (Application Programming Interfaces) that allow frontend and external services to communicate with your application. RESTful APIs, GraphQL, and

WebSocket APIs are common choices. A well-designed API should be intuitive, follow best practices, and provide clear documentation.

Data Management

Managing data is a core function of the backend. Databases like MySQL, PostgreSQL, MongoDB, and Firebase Firestore are commonly used for data storage. Backend developers design and implement database schemas, manage data migrations, and optimize database queries for performance.

Authentication and Authorization

Security is paramount in backend development. Implementing user authentication and authorization mechanisms is critical to protect sensitive data and functionality. Technologies like JSON Web Tokens (JWT) and OAuth2 are commonly used for user authentication and access control.

Middleware

Middleware functions are used to handle various tasks in the backend, such as request validation, logging, and error handling. Middleware can be customized to fit specific project requirements. Popular Node.js frameworks like Express.js make middleware implementation straightforward.

Testing and Debugging

Backend code should be thoroughly tested to ensure it functions correctly. Unit tests, integration tests, and end-to-end tests are common testing strategies. Tools like Postman, Jest, and Mocha assist in backend testing. Debugging tools and logs are essential for identifying and resolving issues.

Scalability and Performance

Backend developers must consider scalability from the outset. Horizontal scaling (adding more servers) and vertical scaling (upgrading server resources) are strategies to handle increased traffic. Caching, load balancing, and optimizing database queries are techniques to improve performance.

API Security

Protecting your API from security threats is vital. Implement security best practices like input validation, rate limiting, and data encryption. Regular security audits and vulnerability assessments help identify and mitigate potential risks.

Documentation

Clear and comprehensive documentation is essential for backend APIs. Tools like Swagger and Postman provide frameworks for generating API documentation. Well-documented APIs simplify integration for frontend developers and third-party services.

In summary, backend development involves selecting the appropriate technology stack, configuring servers, designing APIs, managing data, ensuring security, and optimizing performance. Effective backend development is crucial for delivering a robust and scalable application. In the following section, we'll explore the integration and testing phase of building a real-world project.

Section 17.4: Integration and Testing

Integration and testing are critical phases in the development of a real-world project. These phases ensure that different components of your application work harmoniously and that the final product functions as expected.

Frontend and Backend Integration

The frontend and backend of your application need to integrate seamlessly. Frontend developers often make HTTP requests to backend APIs to fetch and send data. It's essential to define clear API endpoints and adhere to the API contract agreed upon during the planning phase.

Integration testing verifies that the frontend and backend components communicate correctly. It involves testing various scenarios, including successful data retrieval, error handling, and authentication processes. Tools like Postman and Jest are commonly used for integration testing.

Unit Testing

Unit testing focuses on testing individual units or functions in your codebase. Backend developers write unit tests to verify the correctness of their functions and methods. For example, if you have a function that calculates the total price of items in a shopping cart, you would write unit tests to ensure it calculates prices accurately.

Testing frameworks like Mocha, Chai, and Jest provide the tools needed for writing and running unit tests. It's essential to cover various test cases, including edge cases, to ensure code reliability.

End-to-End Testing

End-to-end (E2E) testing examines the entire application workflow from the user's perspective. E2E tests simulate real user interactions with the application. These tests help identify issues that may not be apparent in unit or integration testing.

Tools like Cypress and Selenium are popular choices for E2E testing. E2E tests can include scenarios like user registration, product ordering, and payment processing. They ensure that the entire user journey functions correctly.

Continuous Integration (CI) and Continuous Deployment (CD)

CI/CD pipelines automate the testing and deployment process. They help maintain code quality and ensure that new code changes do not introduce regressions. CI systems like Jenkins, Travis CI, and GitHub Actions can be configured to run automated tests whenever code is pushed to the repository.

Once tests pass successfully in the CI pipeline, CD tools deploy the application to a staging or production environment. This process minimizes manual intervention and reduces the risk of deployment errors.

Load Testing

Load testing evaluates how your application performs under high traffic loads. Backend developers need to ensure that the server can handle a significant number of concurrent users without slowing down or crashing. Load testing tools like Apache JMeter and Artillery can simulate heavy user traffic.

Security Testing

Security testing is an essential part of integration and testing. It involves scanning your application for vulnerabilities, such as SQL injection, cross-site scripting (XSS), and other common security threats. Tools like OWASP ZAP and Nessus can help identify and mitigate security risks.

User Acceptance Testing (UAT)

User acceptance testing involves real users testing the application to ensure it meets their expectations and requirements. Feedback from UAT can reveal usability issues, missing features, or improvements needed to enhance the user experience.

In summary, integration and testing phases are essential for delivering a reliable and secure application. These phases involve integrating frontend and backend components, conducting unit, integration, and end-to-end testing, implementing CI/CD pipelines, load testing, security testing, and user acceptance testing. Successful completion of these phases ensures that your application is ready for deployment and use by your target audience. In the next section, we'll explore the deployment and maintenance aspects of a real-world project.

Section 17.5: Deployment and Maintenance

Deployment and maintenance are the final steps in the development lifecycle of a real-world project. These phases ensure that your application is accessible to users and remains functional and secure over time.

Deployment Strategies

Deployment involves making your application accessible to users. There are several deployment strategies to consider:

1. **Traditional Server Deployment:** In this approach, your application is deployed on one or more physical or virtual servers. You manage server infrastructure, scaling, and maintenance. Popular choices include cloud providers like AWS, Azure, and Google Cloud.

2. **Serverless Deployment:** Serverless computing, offered by platforms like AWS Lambda and Azure Functions, allows you to run code without managing servers. It's cost-effective and auto-scales based on usage.

3. **Containerization:** Docker and container orchestration platforms like Kubernetes enable you to package your application and its dependencies into containers. This approach offers consistency and scalability.

4. **Platform-as-a-Service (PaaS):** PaaS providers like Heroku and Netlify offer a platform for deploying and managing your applications, abstracting infrastructure management.

5. **Content Delivery Networks (CDNs):** CDNs like Cloudflare and Akamai distribute content globally to improve performance and reduce latency.

Continuous Monitoring and Maintenance

Once your application is deployed, continuous monitoring and maintenance are crucial:

1. **Monitoring Tools:** Use monitoring tools like Prometheus, Grafana, or New Relic to track application performance, errors, and user interactions. Monitor server health and resource utilization.

2. **Logging:** Implement structured logging to record important events and errors in your application. Centralized logging solutions like ELK (Elasticsearch, Logstash, Kibana) help analyze logs efficiently.

3. **Incident Response:** Have an incident response plan in place to address issues promptly. Define severity levels, escalation paths, and communication procedures in case of incidents.

4. **Backup and Recovery:** Regularly backup your data and implement disaster recovery plans. Ensure you can restore your application and data in case of unforeseen events.
5. **Security Patching:** Keep all software components up to date, including operating systems, libraries, and dependencies. Apply security patches promptly to protect against vulnerabilities.
6. **Scaling:** Monitor application usage and scale resources as needed to handle increased traffic. Auto-scaling solutions can adjust resource allocation based on demand.
7. **Database Maintenance:** Regularly maintain and optimize databases to ensure data integrity and performance. Implement database backups and redundancy for high availability.
8. **Compliance:** Ensure your application complies with relevant regulations and industry standards, such as GDPR for data protection or PCI DSS for payment processing.

Version Control and Rollback

Version control is critical for tracking changes to your application code. Use Git or other version control systems to manage code changes. Tag releases and maintain a clear release history. In case of issues with a new release, you should be able to rollback to a stable version quickly.

User Support and Feedback

Provide user support channels, such as help desks or community forums, for users to report issues and seek assistance. Collect and analyze user feedback to prioritize feature enhancements and bug fixes.

Documentation

Maintain up-to-date documentation for developers, administrators, and end-users. Proper documentation helps users understand your application, its features, and how to troubleshoot common issues.

End-of-Life Planning

Plan for the end of your application's lifecycle. Define how data will be archived or migrated if the application is retired. Communicate clearly with users about the discontinuation of the service.

In conclusion, deployment and maintenance are critical phases to ensure your real-world project remains accessible, performs well, and stays secure. Consider deployment strategies, continuously monitor your application, plan for incidents, maintain documentation, and be prepared for end-of-life scenarios. Successful maintenance ensures the long-term success of your project and user satisfaction.

Chapter 18: JavaScript Trends and Future

Section 18.1: ECMAScript Evolution

JavaScript, as a language, has evolved significantly over the years. One of the key driving forces behind this evolution is the ECMAScript (ES) specification. ECMAScript is the standardized scripting language specification that JavaScript is based on. Let's explore the evolution of ECMAScript and how it has influenced the JavaScript ecosystem.

A Brief History of ECMAScript

- **ES1 (1997):** The first version of ECMAScript was released alongside the initial release of JavaScript in

Netscape Navigator. It introduced fundamental features like variables, data types, and functions.

- **ES2 (1998):** This version focused on making the specification more precise and added features like exception handling and support for internationalization.

- **ES3 (1999):** ES3 introduced significant improvements, including regular expressions, try/catch exception handling, and better string handling. It became the foundation for JavaScript in web development.

- **ES4 (Abandoned):** The ES4 proposal aimed to introduce major changes to the language, but it faced disagreements among stakeholders and was eventually abandoned.

- **ES5 (2009):** ES5 brought important enhancements like strict mode, JSON support, and various utility methods for arrays and objects. It became widely adopted and formed the basis for many JavaScript libraries.

- **ES6 (ES2015):** A major milestone, ES6 introduced a plethora of new features, including arrow functions, classes, template literals, and promises. It marked a significant shift in JavaScript development.

- **ES2016 and Beyond:** ECMAScript transitioned to a yearly release cycle, introducing smaller but more frequent updates. ES2016 added features like the exponentiation operator, while subsequent versions continued to introduce new capabilities.

Browsers and Compatibility

One challenge in ECMAScript evolution is ensuring compatibility across web browsers. Developers often rely on transpilers like Babel to write modern JavaScript code and compile it to a version compatible with older browsers.

TypeScript and JavaScript Superset

TypeScript, a superset of JavaScript, has gained popularity. It adds static typing and advanced tooling to JavaScript development. Many large-scale projects use TypeScript to catch type-related errors early in development.

ESNext and Future Proposals

The ESNext label refers to the ongoing development of ECMAScript. Proposals are continually being discussed and added to the language. Some notable proposals include optional chaining, pipeline operator, and pattern matching.

Conclusion

ECMAScript's evolution has been instrumental in shaping the JavaScript ecosystem. Developers should stay up-to-date with the latest language features and best practices to leverage the full potential of JavaScript in modern web development. In the next sections of this chapter, we'll explore other trends and technologies that are shaping the future of JavaScript.

Section 18.2: WebAssembly and Beyond

WebAssembly, often abbreviated as wasm, is a binary instruction format that allows running high-performance code on web browsers at near-native speed. While not a part of JavaScript itself, WebAssembly is closely related to JavaScript and has significant implications for the future of web development.

What is WebAssembly?

WebAssembly is a low-level virtual machine that executes code at a binary level. It's designed to be a portable compilation target for high-level programming languages like C, C++, and Rust. This means that developers can write code in these languages and compile it to WebAssembly, which can then run in web browsers. WebAssembly code runs in a secure and sandboxed environment, ensuring that it doesn't pose security risks to users.

Advantages of WebAssembly

1. **Performance:** WebAssembly is designed for high performance, making it suitable for tasks that require heavy computation or real-time processing. It can significantly improve the speed of web applications.
2. **Cross-Platform:** WebAssembly is supported by all major web browsers, including Chrome, Firefox, Safari, and Edge. This ensures cross-browser compatibility.
3. **Language Agnostic:** Developers can write WebAssembly modules in multiple languages, making it a versatile choice for web development.
4. **Web APIs:** WebAssembly can interact seamlessly with JavaScript and access web APIs, allowing developers to

combine the strengths of both technologies.

Use Cases

WebAssembly has various use cases:

- **Gaming:** WebAssembly is well-suited for building browser-based games with high-performance requirements. Game engines like Unity and Unreal Engine can compile to WebAssembly.

- **Multimedia:** Applications that work with audio, video, and image processing can benefit from WebAssembly's performance improvements.

- **Scientific Computing:** Scientific simulations and data analysis can be executed more efficiently in the browser using WebAssembly.

WebAssembly Beyond the Browser

While WebAssembly's primary use case is in web browsers, it has potential applications beyond the web:

- **Server-Side:** Some projects explore using WebAssembly on the server-side for tasks like serverless computing. It allows running the same code on both the client and server, reducing duplication.

- **IoT and Edge Computing:** WebAssembly's small binary size and portability make it suitable for running code on resource-constrained devices in the Internet of Things (IoT) and edge computing scenarios.

Conclusion

WebAssembly represents a significant advancement in web technology, offering high performance and portability. As it continues to evolve, it is likely to play an increasingly important role in web development, enabling developers to build more complex and performant applications both in browsers and on the server-side. Developers should consider learning how to work with WebAssembly to take advantage of its capabilities in their projects.

Section 18.3: Progressive Web Apps (PWAs)

Progressive Web Apps (PWAs) are a modern approach to web application development that aims to combine the best features of web and mobile apps. They provide an enhanced user experience, improved performance, and offline capabilities. PWAs have gained popularity as they allow developers to deliver web applications that feel like native apps across various platforms and devices.

Key Characteristics of PWAs

PWAs exhibit several key characteristics that set them apart from traditional web applications:

1. **Responsive Design:** PWAs are designed to work seamlessly on various screen sizes and orientations, ensuring a consistent experience on desktops, tablets, and smartphones.
2. **Progressive Enhancement:** PWAs are built with progressive enhancement in mind. They work for all users, regardless of the browser or device capabilities. Advanced features are progressively enabled for supporting browsers.
3. **Offline Support:** One of the defining features of PWAs is

their ability to function offline or in low-network conditions. This is achieved through service workers, which cache assets and data, allowing users to access the app even without an internet connection.

4. **App-Like Feel:** PWAs provide a smooth and app-like user experience, including features like smooth animations, gestures, and fullscreen mode. Users can add them to their home screens, making them easily accessible.

5. **Automatic Updates:** PWAs can update themselves in the background, ensuring that users always have the latest version of the app.

6. **Secure:** PWAs are served over HTTPS, ensuring data security and user trust.

Building Blocks of PWAs

To create a Progressive Web App, developers need to consider several key components:

• **Service Workers:** Service workers are JavaScript files that run in the background, intercepting network requests and enabling offline capabilities. They manage caching and provide push notification support.

• **Manifest Files:** PWAs use a manifest file (usually in JSON format) to define the app's name, icons, and other metadata. This allows users to add the app to their home screens.

• **Responsive Design:** A responsive design is essential to ensure that the app looks and works well on various devices and screen sizes.

Benefits of PWAs

PWAs offer numerous benefits to developers and users:

- **Improved User Experience:** PWAs deliver fast loading times, smooth animations, and responsive design, enhancing user satisfaction.

- **Increased Engagement:** Features like push notifications and offline support help engage users and keep them coming back to the app.

- **Reduced Development Effort:** PWAs can be built using web technologies, reducing the need for separate codebases for different platforms.

- **Cost-Effective:** PWAs can be more cost-effective to develop and maintain compared to native apps.

Use Cases for PWAs

PWAs are suitable for a wide range of applications, including:

- E-commerce websites

- News and content platforms

- Social media apps

- Online tools and productivity apps

- Travel and booking services

- Financial and banking apps

Conclusion

Progressive Web Apps have emerged as a powerful approach to web development, offering a blend of web and mobile app features. They provide users with fast, reliable, and engaging experiences, making them a valuable choice for modern web applications. Developers should consider PWAs as an option when building applications that aim to reach a wide audience across different devices and network conditions.

Section 18.4: JavaScript in IoT and Embedded Systems

JavaScript's versatility extends beyond web and mobile app development. It has also found its way into the realm of Internet of Things (IoT) and embedded systems. IoT refers to the interconnection of everyday objects and devices to the internet, allowing them to collect and exchange data. Embedded systems are specialized computing systems integrated into various devices, from household appliances to automotive components. JavaScript's presence in these domains is driven by its ease of use, a rich ecosystem of libraries, and its capacity to handle a wide range of tasks.

JavaScript in IoT

IoT applications often require the ability to collect sensor data, process it, and transmit relevant information to the cloud or other devices. JavaScript has made inroads in IoT for the following reasons:

1. **Node.js for IoT:** Node.js, a JavaScript runtime, is well-suited for IoT applications. It provides non-blocking I/O operations, making it efficient for handling data from sensors and external devices.

2. **Compatibility:** JavaScript can run on microcontrollers, making it possible to develop IoT applications for resource-constrained devices.

3. **IoT Platforms:** Several IoT platforms and frameworks, such as Johnny-Five and Espruino, enable developers to program hardware using JavaScript.

4. **Web APIs:** IoT devices can expose APIs that web applications can interact with. JavaScript's familiarity with web technologies makes it a natural choice for building these applications.

5. **Data Visualization:** JavaScript libraries like D3.js can be used to create interactive data visualizations for IoT data analysis.

JavaScript in Embedded Systems

Embedded systems are at the heart of many devices we use daily, such as smart thermostats, wearable fitness trackers, and automotive control units. JavaScript has found its place in this domain:

1. **Electron:** Electron is a framework for building cross-platform desktop applications using web technologies, including JavaScript. It allows developers to create rich, user-friendly interfaces for embedded applications.

2. **Tessel and Espruino:** Hardware platforms like Tessel and Espruino are designed for developing embedded systems with JavaScript. They provide a JavaScript runtime environment for hardware programming.

3. **Scripting and Automation:** JavaScript is used for scripting and automation in various embedded systems. It can control motors, sensors, and other peripherals, enabling custom functionality.

4. **Web-Based Interfaces:** Many embedded systems include

web-based interfaces for configuration and monitoring. JavaScript plays a key role in creating these interfaces, providing users with a familiar and accessible way to interact with the device.

5. **Real-time Control:** JavaScript's event-driven nature is advantageous for real-time control applications in embedded systems.

Challenges and Considerations

While JavaScript offers advantages in IoT and embedded systems development, there are challenges and considerations:

- **Resource Constraints:** Resource-constrained devices may have limited memory and processing power, which can be a challenge when running JavaScript applications.

- **Security:** Security is paramount, especially in IoT, where devices can be vulnerable to attacks. Developers must follow best practices to secure their JavaScript code and IoT devices.

- **Compatibility:** Ensuring JavaScript code is compatible with various devices and browsers can be challenging, as there is no standard JavaScript runtime for embedded systems.

- **Power Efficiency:** IoT devices often run on battery power. Developers need to optimize their JavaScript code to minimize power consumption.

- **Real-time Requirements:** For real-time applications, JavaScript's garbage collection and asynchronous nature may introduce latency. Careful design is needed to meet real-time constraints.

JavaScript's adoption in IoT and embedded systems reflects its adaptability and the expanding scope of its applications. Developers venturing into these domains should be mindful of the specific requirements and constraints of the devices they are working with, while leveraging JavaScript's strengths to create efficient and innovative solutions.

Section 18.5: The Future of Web Development

The landscape of web development is continually evolving, and JavaScript plays a central role in shaping its future. As we look ahead, several trends and developments are expected to influence the direction of web development in the coming years.

1. WebAssembly (Wasm)

WebAssembly is a binary instruction format that enables high-performance execution of code in web browsers. It allows languages other than JavaScript, such as C++, Rust, and Python, to run in the browser with near-native speed. This technology opens the door to a new era of web applications that can perform complex tasks, such as 3D graphics rendering and scientific simulations, at unprecedented speeds.

```
// Example: Using WebAssembly in JavaScript

fetch('myModule.wasm')

.then(response => response.arrayBuffer())

.then(bytes => WebAssembly.instantiate(bytes))
```

```
.then(results => {

const { instance } = results;

instance.exports.myFunction();

});
```

2. Progressive Web Apps (PWAs)

Progressive Web Apps are web applications that offer a native app-like experience on the web. They work offline, load quickly, and can be installed on users' devices. PWAs leverage technologies like service workers and web app manifests to provide a seamless user experience.

```
// Example: Adding a service worker for offline functionality

if ('serviceWorker' in navigator) {

navigator.serviceWorker.register('sw.js')

.then(registration => {

console.log('Service Worker registered with scope:', registration.scope);

})

.catch(error => {

console.error('Service Worker registration failed:', error);

});

}
```

3. Serverless Computing

Serverless computing allows developers to build and deploy applications without managing the underlying infrastructure. Cloud providers like AWS Lambda, Azure Functions, and Google Cloud Functions enable developers to run code in response to events, reducing operational overhead and cost.

// Example: AWS Lambda function in Node.js

```javascript
exports.handler = async (event) => {

const response = {

statusCode: 200,

body: JSON.stringify('Hello from Lambda!'),

};

return response;

};
```

4. JAMstack Architecture

The JAMstack (JavaScript, APIs, and Markup) architecture is gaining popularity for building fast and secure web applications. It decouples the frontend from the backend, relying on APIs to deliver dynamic content. This approach leads to better performance, security, and scalability.

// Example: Using a static site generator in JAMstack

```javascript
const content = fetch('https://api.example.com/content')

.then(response => response.json());
```

// Render content on the frontend

5. Machine Learning Integration

Machine learning and artificial intelligence are becoming more accessible to web developers. Libraries like TensorFlow.js and tools like Teachable Machine allow developers to incorporate machine learning models into their web applications for tasks like image recognition and natural language processing.

// Example: Using TensorFlow.js for image classification

```
const model = await tf.loadLayersModel('model.json');

const image = document.getElementById('image');

const prediction = await model.predict(image);
```

6. Web 3.0 and Blockchain Integration

Web 3.0 is often associated with decentralized technologies and blockchain integration. This trend aims to create decentralized applications (DApps) that are not controlled by a single entity. Smart contracts, built using languages like Solidity, are central to this movement.

// Example: Interacting with a smart contract in a DApp

```
const contract = new web3.eth.Contract(abi, contractAddress);

const result = await contract.methods.transferTokens(toAddress, amount).send({ from: senderAddress });
```

7. Focus on Web Accessibility and Inclusivity

Web accessibility (a11y) is gaining increased attention. Developers are encouraged to create web applications that are accessible to users with disabilities. This includes adhering to the Web Content Accessibility Guidelines (WCAG) and using ARIA roles to enhance accessibility.

<!—Example: Adding ARIA attributes for screen readers—>

```
<button aria-label="Close" onclick="closeModal()">X</button>
```

8. Cross-Browser Compatibility

Ensuring cross-browser compatibility remains essential as new web technologies emerge. Web developers need to continue testing their applications on various browsers and devices to provide a consistent experience for users.

As web development continues to advance, staying current with these trends and technologies will be crucial for developers. JavaScript, with its versatility and expansive ecosystem, will continue to play a pivotal role in shaping the future of web development. Developers who embrace these trends and adapt to the evolving landscape will be well-positioned for success in the ever-changing world of web development.

Chapter 19: Tips for JavaScript Developers

Section 19.1: Enhancing Productivity with IDEs

Efficiency and productivity are paramount for software developers, and choosing the right Integrated Development Environment (IDE) can significantly impact your workflow. An IDE is a software application that provides a comprehensive set of tools for coding, debugging, and managing projects. In this section, we'll explore the importance of selecting the right IDE and some popular choices for JavaScript development.

Why Choose an IDE?

1. **Code Assistance**: IDEs offer intelligent code completion, highlighting, and suggestions. This helps developers write code faster and with fewer errors.
2. **Debugging Tools**: Debugging is a crucial part of development. IDEs provide powerful debugging features, including breakpoints, variable inspection, and step-by-step execution.
3. **Project Management**: IDEs facilitate project organization by providing project templates, version control integration, and project-wide search and refactoring tools.
4. **Plugin Ecosystem**: Many IDEs have extensive plugin ecosystems that allow you to customize your development environment based on your needs and preferences.

Popular JavaScript IDEs

1. **Visual Studio Code (VS Code):**

– Developed by Microsoft, VS Code is a highly popular, free, and open-source code editor. It offers a rich ecosystem of extensions for JavaScript development.

– Extensions like "ESLint" and "Prettier" help maintain code quality and style.

– Integrated Git support simplifies version control.

1. **WebStorm:**

– WebStorm is a commercial IDE by JetBrains, known for its excellent JavaScript and web development support.

– It provides intelligent coding assistance, advanced debugging, and built-in support for Node.js and popular frameworks like React and Angular.

1. **Atom:**

– Atom is an open-source text editor developed by GitHub. It's highly customizable and extensible through packages.

– Packages like "autocomplete-plus" and "linter-eslint" enhance JavaScript development.

1. **Eclipse with JavaScript Development Tools (JSDT):**

– Eclipse is a popular IDE with a strong Java heritage, but it supports JavaScript development through the JSDT plugin.

– It offers features like content assist, debugging, and integration with popular version control systems.

1. **IntelliJ IDEA:**

– IntelliJ IDEA, also by JetBrains, is renowned for its smart coding assistance and support for JavaScript, TypeScript, and Node.js.

– It includes a wide range of features for efficient development, such as advanced refactoring tools.

IDE Customization

Regardless of the IDE you choose, consider customizing it to align with your workflow. Install relevant extensions or plugins, configure code style rules, and set up key bindings that match your preferences. A well-configured IDE can significantly boost your productivity and make your development experience more enjoyable.

In conclusion, selecting the right IDE is a crucial decision for JavaScript developers. Each IDE has its strengths and weaknesses, so it's essential to evaluate your specific needs and try out different options to find the one that best suits your development style. Whether you prefer lightweight code editors like VS Code or full-fledged IDEs like WebStorm, investing time in setting up and customizing your development environment can lead to substantial productivity gains in your JavaScript projects.

Section 19.2: Version Control and Git Best

Practices

Version control is a fundamental aspect of modern software development, and Git is the most widely used version control system. In this section, we'll explore the importance of version control in JavaScript development and discuss best practices for using Git effectively in your projects.

Why Use Version Control?

Version control allows developers to track changes to their codebase over time, collaborate with others, and ensure the integrity of their project. Here are some key benefits of using version control, especially in JavaScript development:

1. **Change Tracking**: Version control records every change made to your code, enabling you to view the entire history of your project.
2. **Collaboration**: Multiple developers can work on the same project simultaneously without conflicts, thanks to branching and merging capabilities.
3. **Backup and Recovery**: Version control serves as a backup of your code. If something goes wrong, you can revert to a previous state.
4. **Code Review**: It facilitates code reviews by allowing team members to comment on specific code changes and suggest improvements.
5. **Continuous Integration**: Version control systems integrate seamlessly with Continuous Integration (CI) tools, automating the testing and deployment process.

Git Basics

Git is a distributed version control system that offers a range of features for efficient development. Here are some essential Git concepts:

- **Repository (Repo)**: A Git repository is a project's storage space, containing all its files and the history of changes.

- **Commit**: A commit is a snapshot of the code at a specific point in time. Each commit has a unique identifier (SHA-1 hash).

- **Branch**: A branch is a separate line of development in Git. Developers create branches to work on features or bug fixes independently.

- **Merge**: Merging combines changes from one branch into another, typically from a feature branch into the main branch (often named "master" or "main").

Git Best Practices

1. **Use Meaningful Commit Messages**: Write clear and concise commit messages that describe the purpose of the change. A good commit message helps others understand the context.
2. **Frequent Commits**: Make small, frequent commits rather than large, infrequent ones. This makes it easier to track changes and collaborate effectively.
3. **Branching Strategy**: Adopt a branching strategy that suits your project. Common strategies include "feature branching" and "Gitflow."

4. **Pull Requests**: If using a platform like GitHub or GitLab, create pull requests (or merge requests) for code review before merging changes into the main branch.
5. **.gitignore**: Utilize a .gitignore file to specify which files or directories should be excluded from version control, such as build artifacts or sensitive configuration files.
6. **Rebase vs. Merge**: Understand the difference between rebasing and merging. Rebasing can create a linear history, while merging preserves branch history.
7. **Push and Pull Frequently**: Regularly push your local changes to the remote repository to avoid conflicts and keep your branch up-to-date.
8. **Code Reviews**: Encourage code reviews within your team. Code reviews help maintain code quality and catch issues early.
9. **Tagging Releases**: Use tags to mark specific commits as releases. This makes it easy to reference stable versions of your software.
10. **Documentation**: Keep your project's README and documentation up-to-date. Include information on how to set up and run the project.

In summary, version control with Git is essential for JavaScript developers to manage code changes, collaborate effectively, and maintain project integrity. By following best practices like meaningful commit messages, branching strategies, and code reviews, you can streamline your development workflow and ensure the success of your JavaScript projects.

Section 19.3: Learning Resources and Communities

As a JavaScript developer, continuous learning is essential to stay updated with the rapidly evolving JavaScript ecosystem and to enhance your skills. In this section, we will explore various learning resources and communities that can help you on your journey to becoming a proficient JavaScript developer.

Online Learning Platforms

1. **Coursera**: Coursera offers a wide range of JavaScript courses from top universities and institutions. You can learn at your own pace and earn certificates upon completion.
2. **edX**: Similar to Coursera, edX provides access to high-quality JavaScript courses from universities and colleges worldwide. Many courses are free, with an option to receive a verified certificate for a fee.
3. **Udemy**: Udemy hosts numerous JavaScript courses created by industry professionals. You can find courses on various topics, from beginner to advanced levels.
4. **Codecademy**: Codecademy offers interactive coding lessons in JavaScript and other programming languages. It's a great platform for hands-on practice.
5. **FreeCodeCamp**: FreeCodeCamp is a nonprofit organization that provides free, self-paced JavaScript curriculum, along with projects and certifications. It also has an active community.

Books

1. **"Eloquent JavaScript" by Marijn Haverbeke**: This

popular online book is available for free and covers JavaScript fundamentals and advanced concepts.

2. **"You Don't Know JS" by Kyle Simpson**: This book series delves deep into JavaScript, explaining complex topics in an accessible way.

3. **"JavaScript: The Good Parts" by Douglas Crockford**: This classic book focuses on the best practices and the "good parts" of JavaScript.

Documentation and References

1. **Mozilla Developer Network (MDN)**: MDN provides comprehensive documentation for JavaScript, including guides, reference material, and tutorials.

2. **W3Schools**: W3Schools offers tutorials and references for JavaScript and web development technologies.

3. **JavaScript MDN Web Docs**: This documentation specifically focuses on JavaScript and is an excellent resource for understanding language features and APIs.

Coding Challenges and Practice

1. **LeetCode**: LeetCode offers coding challenges in JavaScript and other languages. It's a great platform to improve your problem-solving skills.

2. **HackerRank**: HackerRank provides JavaScript challenges and competitions, allowing you to practice and compete with other developers.

Online Communities

1. **Stack Overflow**: Stack Overflow is a vast community of developers where you can ask questions, seek solutions to

coding problems, and contribute by answering others' questions.

2. **GitHub**: GitHub is a platform for hosting and collaborating on open-source projects. It's also a place to discover and contribute to JavaScript libraries and frameworks.

3. **Reddit JavaScript Community**: The r/javascript subreddit is a place for JavaScript enthusiasts to share news, ask questions, and engage in discussions.

4. **Dev.to**: Dev.to is a platform for developers to share articles, tutorials, and insights. It has a vibrant JavaScript community.

Meetups and Conferences

1. **Meetup.com**: Use Meetup to find local JavaScript meetups and events where you can network with other developers and attend tech talks.

2. **JavaScript Conferences**: Consider attending JavaScript conferences like JSConf, ReactConf, or NodeConf to learn from industry leaders and connect with fellow developers.

YouTube Channels and Podcasts

1. **The Net Ninja**: This YouTube channel offers high-quality JavaScript tutorials and web development content.

2. **JavaScript Jabber Podcast**: Listen to JavaScript experts discuss various topics related to web development and JavaScript.

Remember that learning is an ongoing process, and staying connected with the JavaScript community can provide valuable insights, support, and opportunities for collaboration. Whether you prefer online courses, books, coding challenges, or community engagement, there are plenty of resources available to help you excel in your JavaScript development journey.

Section 19.4: Staying Updated in the JavaScript Ecosystem

In the ever-evolving world of JavaScript, staying updated with the latest trends, tools, and best practices is crucial to remain competitive and produce high-quality code. In this section, we'll explore strategies for staying informed about JavaScript developments.

Newsletters and Blogs

1. **JavaScript Weekly**: Subscribe to newsletters like JavaScript Weekly to receive curated news, articles, and resources in your inbox regularly.
2. **Medium**: Many JavaScript experts and developers share their knowledge and insights through articles on Medium. Follow relevant publications and authors to keep up with the latest trends.
3. **Dev.to**: The Dev.to platform hosts a variety of articles and discussions related to JavaScript. You can follow tags and authors to customize your feed.

Twitter and Social Media

1. **Twitter**: Follow JavaScript influencers, developers, and organizations on Twitter. Twitter is a great platform for real-time updates and discussions. Use hashtags like #JavaScript and #WebDev.
2. **LinkedIn**: LinkedIn is another valuable platform for professional networking. Join JavaScript-related groups

and follow industry leaders.

Podcasts and YouTube Channels

1. **JavaScript Podcasts**: There are several podcasts dedicated to JavaScript, such as JavaScript Jabber and JavaScript Air. Listen to episodes during your commute or while coding.
2. **YouTube Channels**: YouTube hosts numerous channels with tutorials, conference talks, and updates on JavaScript and web development.

GitHub Trends and Repositories

1. **GitHub Explore**: Visit the GitHub Explore section to discover trending JavaScript repositories. This can help you find new libraries, frameworks, and tools.
2. **GitHub Notifications**: Use GitHub's notification feature to keep track of updates in repositories you're interested in. You can receive notifications for new releases, issues, and pull requests.

Conferences and Meetups

1. **Virtual Conferences**: Many conferences offer virtual attendance options, making it easier to access expert talks and presentations from around the world.
2. **Local Meetups**: Attend local JavaScript meetups and user groups. These events often feature speakers who discuss the latest advancements in the field.

Online Courses and Learning Platforms

1. **Coursera and edX**: Explore courses on Coursera and edX

that cover advanced JavaScript topics and emerging trends in web development.

2. **Udemy**: Udemy regularly updates its course offerings, so you can find courses that teach the latest JavaScript frameworks and libraries.

Books and Publications

1. **Ebooks and Epubs**: Consider digital books and publications that offer timely insights into JavaScript trends. Ebooks can be updated more frequently than print books.
2. **Technical Magazines**: Some technical magazines, both in print and digital formats, feature articles on JavaScript's latest developments.

Industry Reports

1. **State of JavaScript**: The "State of JavaScript" survey and report are published annually, providing insights into popular libraries, frameworks, and tools.
2. **GitHub's Octoverse**: GitHub releases its Octoverse report, highlighting the most popular and trending repositories and technologies.

Online Courses and Certifications

1. **JavaScript Certifications**: Enroll in advanced JavaScript courses and certifications on platforms like Coursera and edX to deepen your knowledge and skills.
2. **Bootcamps**: Consider joining coding bootcamps focused on the latest web development technologies, including JavaScript frameworks.

By combining multiple sources and staying engaged with the JavaScript community, you can ensure that you're always aware of the latest developments and trends. Regularly setting aside time for learning and staying informed will contribute to your growth as a JavaScript developer.

Section 19.5: Career Opportunities and Growth

In the world of JavaScript development, career opportunities are abundant, and growth potential is vast. Whether you're just starting your journey or looking to advance in your career, this section explores various aspects of career development and growth in the field of JavaScript.

1. Diverse Career Paths

JavaScript developers can follow diverse career paths, including front-end, back-end, full-stack, and specialized roles such as UI/UX developer, mobile app developer, or DevOps engineer. Your career path can be tailored to your interests and strengths.

2. Continuous Learning

Staying updated with the latest JavaScript trends and technologies is essential. JavaScript evolves rapidly, and continuous learning is key to remaining competitive. Consider pursuing online courses, certifications, and attending workshops or conferences to enhance your skills.

3. Contributing to Open Source

Contributing to open-source projects is an excellent way to gain experience, collaborate with experienced developers, and showcase your skills. Platforms like GitHub provide opportunities to make meaningful contributions to the JavaScript community.

4. Building a Portfolio

Create a portfolio of your projects, including personal websites, web apps, or contributions to open-source projects. A well-documented portfolio can impress potential employers and clients.

5. Networking

Networking plays a crucial role in career growth. Attend meetups, conferences, and online forums to connect with other developers and potential employers. LinkedIn is a valuable platform for professional networking.

6. Job Market

The job market for JavaScript developers remains strong. Companies of all sizes seek JavaScript expertise for web development, mobile app development, and server-side development using technologies like Node.js.

7. Remote Work Opportunities

JavaScript developers often have the flexibility to work remotely. Remote work opportunities have expanded in recent years, allowing developers to collaborate with teams worldwide.

8. Freelancing and Consulting

Many JavaScript developers choose to work as freelancers or consultants. This path offers independence, flexibility, and the opportunity to work on a variety of projects.

9. Soft Skills

In addition to technical skills, soft skills like communication, problem-solving, and teamwork are highly valued in the tech industry. Developing these skills can enhance your career prospects.

10. Salary Growth

Experienced JavaScript developers command competitive salaries. As you gain expertise and experience, your earning potential increases significantly.

11. Mentorship and Coaching

Consider seeking mentorship from experienced developers or joining coaching programs. Mentorship can provide valuable guidance and accelerate your career growth.

12. Career Transitions

JavaScript is a versatile language, and it's possible to transition into JavaScript development from other fields or to move from JavaScript into other tech roles.

13. Job Satisfaction

Many JavaScript developers find their work rewarding and fulfilling. Solving complex problems, building innovative solutions, and seeing your work in action can be highly satisfying.

14. Work-Life Balance

The tech industry often offers good work-life balance, with flexible hours and the option to work remotely, allowing you to maintain a healthy work-life balance.

15. Diversity and Inclusion

Efforts are underway in the tech industry to improve diversity and inclusion. Developers from diverse backgrounds are encouraged to contribute and help shape the future of technology.

In conclusion, the world of JavaScript development is full of opportunities for career growth and personal development. Whether you're starting your journey or looking to advance, continuous learning, networking, and building a strong portfolio are key to a successful and fulfilling career in JavaScript. Embrace the challenges, stay curious, and keep pushing the boundaries of what you can achieve as a JavaScript developer.

Chapter 20: Conclusion and Beyond

Section 20.1: Recap of Key Concepts

In this final chapter of our JavaScript journey, we'll recap the key concepts and takeaways from this comprehensive guide. This section serves as a summary of the knowledge and skills you've acquired throughout the book.

1. JavaScript Fundamentals

- You've learned the core concepts of JavaScript, including variables, data types, operators, control structures, and functions. These form the foundation of any JavaScript development.

2. DOM Manipulation

- Understanding the Document Object Model (DOM) is crucial for web development. You can select and manipulate HTML elements, handle events, and create interactive web pages.

3. Advanced JavaScript

- You've delved into advanced topics like closures, prototypes, asynchronous programming with promises, and error handling. These concepts are essential for writing maintainable and efficient code.

4. Front-End Libraries and Frameworks

- You've explored popular libraries like jQuery and modern frameworks like React, Angular, and Vue.js. These tools empower you to build dynamic and responsive user interfaces.

5. Server-Side JavaScript

- Node.js enables server-side JavaScript development. You've learned how to create APIs, work with databases, and build real-time applications using WebSocket.

6. Data Handling and Visualization

- JavaScript allows you to work with JSON data, consume RESTful APIs, and visualize data using libraries like D3.js. These skills are valuable for data-centric applications.

7. Security and Best Practices

- Understanding security threats and implementing best practices, such as XSS prevention and CSRF protection, is crucial for safeguarding web applications.

8. Testing and Debugging

- You've explored unit testing with Mocha and Chai, debugging techniques, performance profiling, and code quality through continuous integration and code reviews.

9. Single-Page Applications (SPAs)

- SPAs offer a seamless user experience. You've learned about routing, state management with Redux, and building SPAs using React and best practices.

10. Mobile App Development

- You've gained insights into mobile app development using technologies like React Native, Ionic, and Progressive Web Apps (PWAs). These approaches allow you to reach a broader audience.

11. Web Performance Optimization

- Performance optimization is vital for user satisfaction. You've explored techniques for loading, rendering, network optimization, and measuring performance.

12. Accessibility

- Building accessible web interfaces ensures inclusivity. You've learned about web accessibility principles, assistive technologies, and ARIA roles.

13. Internationalization and Localization

- JavaScript's Intl API enables you to create multilingual applications. You've explored techniques for language detection, localization, and handling regional preferences.

14. Advanced JavaScript Topics

- You've been introduced to web components, serverless computing with AWS Lambda, WebAssembly, machine learning, and blockchain integration, showcasing the breadth of JavaScript applications.

15. Real-World Project

- Building a real-world project involves planning, frontend and backend development, integration, testing, and deployment—a holistic view of software development.

16. JavaScript Trends and Future

- You've glimpsed into the future of JavaScript, including ECMAScript evolution, WebAssembly, Progressive Web Apps, IoT, and embedded systems.

17. Tips for JavaScript Developers

- Enhancing productivity with IDEs, version control with Git, leveraging learning resources and communities, staying updated, and exploring career opportunities are essential for your growth.

18. Conclusion and Beyond

- This chapter marks the end of the book, but it's just the beginning of your JavaScript journey. Embrace change in web development, continue learning, and explore the vast possibilities that JavaScript offers.

In conclusion, JavaScript is a versatile and powerful language that underpins modern web development. Whether you're a beginner or an experienced developer, the knowledge and skills you've gained from this book equip you to tackle a wide range of web development challenges. Your journey as a JavaScript developer is an ongoing adventure, and the possibilities are endless. Thank you for joining us on this educational journey, and we wish you success in all your JavaScript endeavors!

Section 20.2: The Journey of Becoming a JavaScript Expert

Becoming an expert in JavaScript, or any programming language, is a journey that requires dedication, continuous learning, and practical experience. In this section, we'll explore the path to becoming a JavaScript expert and offer guidance on how to progress in your career as a developer.

1. Master the Fundamentals

- The foundation of expertise lies in mastering the basics. Ensure you have a deep understanding of JavaScript's core concepts, including variables, data types, functions, and control structures. Continually practice and reinforce these fundamentals.

2. Explore Advanced Topics

- To reach the expert level, delve into advanced JavaScript topics such as closures, prototypes, asynchronous programming, and error handling. These concepts are essential for writing efficient and maintainable code.

3. Build Real-World Projects

- Apply your knowledge by working on real-world projects. Building applications from scratch or contributing to open-source projects allows you to gain practical experience and learn from real challenges.

4. Deepen Your Web Development Skills

- JavaScript is often just one part of web development. Learn about HTML, CSS, and web design principles to become a well-rounded developer capable of creating complete web solutions.

5. Explore Frameworks and Libraries

- JavaScript's ecosystem is rich with frameworks and libraries. Explore these tools to streamline development and stay updated with industry trends. Whether it's React, Angular, Vue.js, or others, understanding their use cases can be invaluable.

6. Practice Problem Solving

- Becoming an expert developer requires strong problem-solving skills. Regularly challenge yourself with coding problems and algorithm challenges on platforms like LeetCode and HackerRank.

7. Contribute to Open Source

- Open-source contributions not only benefit the community but also enhance your skills. Participate in open-source projects, submit bug fixes, or create your projects for others to use.

8. Stay Updated

- JavaScript and web development are continuously evolving. Keep up with the latest updates, new features, and best practices by reading blogs, following industry experts on social media, and attending conferences or meetups.

9. Peer Collaboration and Code Reviews

• Collaborating with peers and participating in code reviews can significantly improve your skills. Learn from others' code and provide constructive feedback.

10. Teach and Share Knowledge

- Teaching is one of the most effective ways to solidify your understanding. Share your knowledge by writing blog posts, creating tutorials, or mentoring others.

11. Networking and Community Involvement

- Join developer communities, attend conferences, and network with fellow developers. These connections can lead to learning opportunities and potential collaborations.

12. Adapt to Industry Trends

- The tech industry is ever-changing. Be adaptable and open to exploring new technologies and paradigms. This flexibility will keep you relevant in the field.

13. Certifications and Formal Education

- Consider pursuing relevant certifications or formal education, such as a computer science degree or online courses. These can provide structured learning and validation of your skills.

14. Continuous Learning

- The path to expertise is never-ending. Embrace a mindset of continuous learning, and never stop seeking ways to improve your skills and stay at the forefront of your field.

Becoming a JavaScript expert is not a destination but a journey of growth and improvement. It requires dedication, passion, and a commitment to lifelong learning. As you progress on this journey, remember that expertise is not measured by what you know but by how effectively you can apply that knowledge to solve real-world problems. Embrace the challenges, celebrate your successes, and stay curious, for the world of JavaScript development is both dynamic and rewarding.

Section 20.3: Embracing Change in Web Development

Web development is a dynamic field that evolves rapidly. As a JavaScript developer, embracing change is not just a recommendation; it's a necessity. In this section, we'll explore how to adapt to changes in web development, stay updated, and thrive in this ever-changing environment.

1. Keep Learning New Technologies

- The web development landscape is constantly evolving with new libraries, frameworks, and tools. Stay curious and dedicate time to learning about emerging technologies. Don't shy away from exploring new languages or paradigms.

2. Follow Industry Trends

- Stay informed about industry trends and best practices by reading blogs, watching tech talks, and following influential figures on social media. Twitter and LinkedIn can be valuable sources of information.

3. Attend Conferences and Meetups

- Participate in conferences, meetups, and webinars related to web development. These events offer insights into the latest trends, networking opportunities, and chances to learn from experts.

4. Engage with Online Communities

- Join online communities, forums, and developer groups where you can ask questions, share knowledge, and discuss new technologies. Platforms like Stack Overflow, Reddit, and GitHub are excellent places to engage.

5. Regularly Update Your Skills

- Dedicate time for skill updates. Revisit your existing projects to apply new techniques, and consider refactoring to incorporate the latest best practices.

6. Experiment with New Features

- Explore browser features and APIs as they evolve. Experimenting with new features and APIs can lead to innovative solutions in your projects.

7. Stay Security Conscious

- Web security is an ever-present concern. Keep up with security best practices and vulnerabilities to ensure your applications remain safe.

8. Adopt Agile and DevOps Practices

- Agile methodologies and DevOps practices can help you adapt quickly to changing requirements and streamline development workflows.

9. Learn from Mistakes

- Mistakes are part of the learning process. When things don't go as planned, use it as an opportunity to learn and improve. Don't be afraid to iterate and refactor.

10. Collaborate and Seek Feedback

- Collaboration with peers and seeking feedback can provide fresh perspectives and insights. Code reviews and pair programming can lead to better solutions.

11. Build a Personal Brand

- Share your knowledge and experiences through blogging, social media, or speaking engagements. Building a personal brand can establish you as an expert in your field.

12. Explore Cross-Platform Development

- As the demand for cross-platform solutions grows, consider learning technologies like React Native, Flutter, or Xamarin to build mobile applications using your JavaScript skills.

13. Adapt to Browser Updates

- Browsers continuously update their standards and features. Stay informed about changes and ensure your web applications remain compatible.

14. Migrate Legacy Code

- If you work with legacy codebases, have a plan to modernize them. Migrating to newer technologies and best practices can extend the life of your projects.

15. Embrace the JavaScript Ecosystem

- JavaScript is not limited to the browser; it's also used in server-side development, IoT, and more. Explore these areas to diversify your skill set.

16. Enjoy the Journey

- Embracing change in web development is an ongoing journey. Enjoy the process of learning, adapting, and innovating. The challenges you face today will lead to growth and opportunities tomorrow.

In the fast-paced world of web development, adaptability and a willingness to learn are your greatest assets. Embrace change as an opportunity for growth, and you'll not only stay relevant but also excel in your career as a JavaScript developer. Remember that change is a constant, and those who embrace it are the ones who shape the future of web development.

Section 20.4: Your Next Steps as a JavaScript Developer

Congratulations on completing this comprehensive guide to JavaScript! As you wrap up your journey through this book, you might be wondering about your next steps as a JavaScript developer. This section offers guidance on how to continue your growth and build a successful career in web development.

1. Specialize or Diversify

- Decide whether you want to specialize in a particular area of web development, such as front-end, back-end, full-stack, or mobile app development. Alternatively, you can choose to diversify your skills across multiple domains. Your choice depends on your interests and career goals.

2. Build a Portfolio

- Create a portfolio of projects that showcase your skills and expertise. A portfolio is an invaluable asset when applying for jobs or freelance opportunities. Include a variety of projects to demonstrate your versatility.

3. Open Source Contributions

- Consider contributing to open source projects. Collaborating with the open source community not only enhances your coding skills but also allows you to work on real-world projects and gain recognition among peers.

4. Continued Learning

- Web development is an ever-evolving field. Keep learning by exploring new technologies, libraries, and frameworks. Online courses, tutorials, and documentation are excellent resources for self-paced learning.

5. Networking

- Networking is crucial for career growth. Attend meetups, conferences, and webinars to connect with fellow developers and industry professionals. Online platforms like LinkedIn and GitHub can also help you expand your professional network.

6. Job Search and Freelancing

- If you're seeking employment, tailor your resume and cover letter to highlight your skills and experiences relevant to the positions you're applying for. For those interested in freelancing, platforms like Upwork and Freelancer offer opportunities to find projects.

7. Certifications

- Consider obtaining certifications in web development or related fields. Certifications can validate your skills and make you more attractive to potential employers.

8. Stay Updated

- Stay informed about industry trends, best practices, and emerging technologies. Subscribe to newsletters, follow tech blogs, and engage with the developer community to stay up to date.

9. Soft Skills

• Developing soft skills such as communication, teamwork, problem-solving, and time management is equally important. These skills can set you apart in the workplace.

10. Mentorship

- Seek mentorship from experienced developers. A mentor can provide guidance, share insights, and help you navigate your career path.

11. Side Projects

- Work on side projects that align with your interests. These projects allow you to experiment, learn, and apply new technologies in a real-world context.

12. Consider Advanced Topics

- If you're ready for a deeper dive, explore advanced topics such as machine learning, blockchain, or serverless computing, depending on your interests.

13. Contribute to the Community

- Give back to the developer community by sharing your knowledge through blogging, creating tutorials, or speaking at events. Teaching others can solidify your understanding of the material and help fellow developers.

14. Evaluate Job Offers

- When you receive job offers, carefully evaluate them based on factors like salary, benefits, company culture, and growth opportunities. Choose a role that aligns with your career goals.

15. Set Goals

- Set clear, achievable goals for your career. Whether it's landing a specific job, starting your own business, or mastering a new technology, having goals provides direction and motivation.

Remember that your journey as a JavaScript developer is ongoing. Embrace challenges, stay curious, and adapt to the ever-changing web development landscape. Your dedication to continuous learning and improvement will lead to a rewarding and fulfilling career in this dynamic field.

Section 20.5: Thank You and Acknowledgments

As we conclude this comprehensive guide to JavaScript, I want to express my heartfelt gratitude to all the readers who embarked on this journey. Learning JavaScript and web development is a significant endeavor, and your dedication to expanding your knowledge is commendable.

I also want to extend my appreciation to the individuals and communities that make the world of web development vibrant and supportive. The open source contributors, educators, bloggers, and experts who tirelessly share their knowledge have played an instrumental role in shaping the JavaScript ecosystem.

I would like to acknowledge the authors and creators of the tools, libraries, and frameworks discussed throughout this book. Their innovation and commitment to improving web development have enriched the experiences of developers worldwide.

Additionally, I want to thank the team at [Your Publishing Company] for their efforts in bringing this book to fruition. Their dedication to providing quality educational resources is evident in every page.

Lastly, I encourage you to keep your passion for web development alive. The journey doesn't end here; it continues as you explore new technologies, tackle exciting projects, and contribute to the ever-evolving world of JavaScript.

Thank you for choosing this book as your companion on your JavaScript learning path. I wish you all the success and fulfillment in your career as a JavaScript developer. If you ever have questions or seek guidance in the future, remember that the JavaScript community is always here to support you.

Happy coding!